Wealth DNA:
The Master Entrepreneur:

Cracking the Code to Massive Wealth

Second Edition

Lee Christopher Grant

WealthGate Publishing Company
43193 Thistledown Terrace, Suite 327
Ashburn, VA 20148

WealthGate, LLC

Head Office:
43193 Thistledown Terrace, Suite 327
Ashburn, VA 20148

Website: www.visualcv.com/wealthdna

First published in United States 2004

TABLE OF CONTENTS

ACKNOWLEDGMENTS

I've been influenced by many people, and it would take the pages in this book to list them all, but there are some key people who have made a big impact on me.

I'll start with my mother and father, who never wavered in their belief in my potential. To Claudine Brown, a woman who many years ago recognized my true calling as an entrepreneurial consultant (she was the first entrepreneur I ever met). To Renard Hurns and Edward Collum, friends and colleagues who epitomize what being "self-made" is all about. To all of my present and past clients, who allowed me to create value for them. To Aslan Mirkalami, Akhil Thapliyal, Nancy Curtis and Art Sands, four entrepreneurs who were gracious enough to allow me to share their stories here.

To the genius of Buffet, Munger, Getty, Onassis, Ghandi, Sun Tzu, U.S. Andersen, Mobius, Tracy, and Winfrey—all contributed in someway in shaping my thinking. And finally to my extended family of close-knit colleagues, who continue to support and inspire me.

To all, I say: *thank you.*

Introduction

"The great thing in this world is not so much where we are, but in what direction we are moving."
~ Oliver Wendell Holmes

Entrepreneurs…Intrapreneurs…Risk takers…welcome. You are among the most rare group of people on the planet; people who strive to design, build or run something that succeeds because of your passion, inner drive and focus.

For some of you, you may just be starting out. Welcome. It's exciting, isn't it? For others, you're well into the thick of things; perhaps working on your second, third or fourth venture.

We're constantly defying the odds, aren't we? Our friends and families, while encouraging, probably think that what we do is terrifying, crazy even. For some of you it probably has been at times. But how could it be any other way? When we were employees, we were constantly pushing the envelope, never failing to have that bright idea or two, causing our supervisors to scratch their heads with wonder, amazement and for some—frustration. Frustration because we were constantly pushing the boundaries, testing, breaking or outright ignoring "the rules." Status quo isn't good enough, and we wanted opportunities and rewards. Grow or die we say, right?

In fact, for many of us, myself included, we started our adventure as intrapreneurs. Working for an employer, we usually contributed to the organization far over our employment duties. For some, the motivation was money or to be upwardly mobile, but for others it's just the way we ran. And when the employer couldn't offer us any new opportunities to conquer, we ventured out on our own. Sometimes carefully and wisely, sometimes recklessly, but always counting on our inner drive and passion to keep us safe.

The entrepreneurial gene can be inherent in a person. Many events can trigger it, but the three most common triggers are: (1) active nurturing; (2) responding to a personal crisis (loss of income) or sudden opportunity; (3) learned behavior. Regardless of what put you on this path, to all we say welcome aboard.

In this book, we have much ground to cover, ideas to discuss and think about, and I think you will enjoy reading it. One skill entrepreneurs are good at is creating the leverage necessary to get the result they're shooting for. This book is no exception. I created massive leverage designed to help me write, complete and craft a book that was enjoyable to read. This leverage occurred when I decided to create my own "advisory board." This board consisted of individuals who I trusted and respected, who would be willing to tell me the truth versus what I wanted to hear. They knew I wanted to create a great book, and their critical (but helpful) comments led to seven drafts, resulting in the best book I could produce at the time I wrote this.

The result is a book that stretches your thinking and engages your imagination; a book that will serve as a field manual for all entrepreneurs and intrapreneurs alike. I'll let you be the judge of that.

Obviously, I want you to find the book both interesting and readable, but I also wanted to offer strategies for creating balance in your life. For you veteran entrepreneurs out there, you already know how important it is to live a life in balance. You already know it's more important than money itself.

For those of you just starting out, I am honored to be able to share this book with you. If my experience and those of others offered in this book creates value for you, then I've already succeeded. In fact, that's what this book is about, being a success.

"The vision must be followed by the venture.
It is not enough to stare up the steps—we must step up the stairs"
~ Vance Havner

Why write this book?

I am a voracious reader. Last checked, I've read over 700 books and I'm just shy 40 years old. Of this, I've looked at several hundred books, articles, tapes related to business, business development, and strategy. However, in all this time I have never seen a book that discussed the different types of entrepreneurs needed by a growing business. Yes, I've seen books discussing business cycles and I've seen books discussing what it's like being an entrepreneur, but never in the same book.

It's said that there's nothing new under the sun, the newness of an idea is how information is combined, shaped, presented and how relevant this "new idea" is to the challenges and problems currently faced.

This book focuses on the core thinking and actions that successful entrepreneurs have when designing, building, continuing or buying an enterprise. This is not an excessively technical book, in that I do not spend time on the technical specifics of business formation, legal, accounting, or tax issues. There are many excellent books that address these specific areas. Instead, the book focuses on what *being* a successful entrepreneur looks like and what setting up and running a successful enterprise looks like. This book covers what I call the basic DNA of the master entrepreneur and superior enterprise.

Many of the ideas introduced are based on principles, which are old— in many cases, hundreds of years old. What I offer you is my particular cocktail. Of course there are many variations possible, but take this one for a spin, will you?

Also, I welcome your comments and suggestions. If you have any to share with me, please send them to me at the following e-mail address:

<u>Wealthdna@gmail.com</u>

■ ■

To keep this book from being a 500-page treatise, I've created a website with updates to some of the information published. I invite you to come and see the information that is there.

The team at Visualcv.com was kind enough to create this environment for you. The site's address is:

www.visualcv.com/wealthdna

How to use this book

The book takes you through a steady progression. It quickly begins with defining key ideas: The characteristics of the Master Entrepreneur, the four entrepreneurial types and the business growth cycle of the Superior Enterprise. This is Part I of the book. Part II delves deeper into the profile of each entrepreneurial type, and what they contribute at various stages of business growth.

In Part II I introduce you to several entrepreneurs who were kind enough to offer the wisdom of their experience and advice.

When you finish reading, you'll have a sound understanding of exactly which entrepreneur you're naturally inclined to be. But perhaps more importantly, you'll be able to recognize other entrepreneurial types easily and will have a better sense of the types of teams needed to build at each stage of your business' life. Unique to small business owners is the fact the majority running small businesses has had to play all 4 roles. From reading this book, you will be able to discover the role that most closely resonates with you. And finally, we'll discuss the mindset of the "Investor," and what investors are looking for, and more importantly, what you should expect from them. When I'm done, you will never again fear approaching investors for capital, because you will be doing so with the right mindset.

So, get comfortable, settle into your favorite chair and let's get started, shall we?

The DNA of the Master Entrepreneur

"The greatest discovery of my generation is that human beings can alter their lives by altering their attitudes of mind."
—William James

Wealth DNA. Cute title, but what does it mean? Well, the meaning is symbolic and it's meant to serve as a metaphor, an anchor, a reminder that the root of all wealth creation begins first in the mind and spirit. The human brain has ten billion brain cells and we only use a fraction, a small fraction of our intellectual ability. I believe wealth begins with a thought and that what you focus on and what you persist in thinking about, becomes real.

The mind is powerful. I remember as a small child, how, with just a few questions from my mother, I could manifest illness quickly. Something as simple as a runny nose and slight fever, with just a few series of questions, turns into something serious like the flu. To this day, when my Mother asks, me how I am feeling, I always answer the question with "fantastic!"

Wealth creation works the same way. If one focuses on what he doesn't have, concentrates on not having enough money, tells himself there isn't enough of this or that and there is no possibility of attracting more, of attracting enough-then that's what you'll have. Instead of saying "I can't afford it," ask, "how might I be able to afford this?"—Give that powerful mind a target to shoot at.

To create a new business is to create new wealth

Entrepreneurs are constantly setting targets and shooting at it. We ask ourselves "what can I do?" "How can I get it done?" It's a rare moment that we'll spend anytime at all making self-defeating statements like "I can't see a way we can do this." Doing the impossible is as simple as breathing for us, and if something has even the slightest chance of paying off, we will most likely give it some consideration—and often chase it.

For many it looks foolish; we're seen as risk takers, gamblers and lunatics. Still, when we get it right, suddenly we are visionaries, geniuses, wizards and heroes. Regardless of how you became an entrepreneur, you're wired to work this way.

And it's something you should celebrate: entrepreneurs are the trailblazers of innovation, and are often at the center of wealth creation in the world.

The Three levels of Money creation

There are many ways to create wealth in one's life, and with monetary wealth, there are three levels:

- **M1 Money**: your direct efforts (time, labor, and focus) produce money for you.

- **M2 Money**: the direct efforts (time, labor, focus) of others produce money for you.

- **M3 Money**: your money (assets, investments) produces money for you.

The M1 Money state is the most common on earth. You have a job, maybe you're self-employed, a one-person business or a freelance consultant even. In every case, money results from your direct efforts, your direct labor. Your compensation is directly proportional to your energy output-no more, no less.

Interesting enough, in the United States, people working in the M1 realm pay the most in taxes. Ironically, those who can most easily afford to pay taxes (business owners and wealthy individuals) pay the least taxes. Whenever someone asks me "Chris, what's the best way to become rich?" I usually answer with, "Find a way to keep most of what you earn." And normally, that means getting involved with business opportunities that create tax advantages to you. Starting a business falls in that category.

The M1 state is the riskiest way to live, and it's often the most expensive. Expensive not only in the tax department, but also in the time you have to devote to the JOB; time you can't spend with family and loved ones; the vacations missed, for example.

People in the M1 state incur other potential "losses" as well: losses involving missed opportunities. It is the most expensive and riskiest way to create the life you want to live now and in the future. Most people living in an M1 state dream of a better future but haven't taken the actions necessary to make those dreams happen. Money earned somehow just covers the bills but not much else. Ironically, it is the easiest way to exist, since having a job is what most societies encourage for their people.

And for people who are in the upper-middle class income bracket it gets even more interesting. Their salary level makes them eligible to borrow too much money, to buy too much car, too much house—too much of everything. I've known a few people who earn $80,000 to $120,000 a year and they are broke, trapped in this huge life-style that they built mostly on debt.

I'm willing to place a small wager that most of the readers of this book can identify with this, and for some of you, it's probably what drove you to consider the entrepreneur route in the first place. You wanted out of the Rat Race, right? I know I did.

When creating a business, a service-related business, you are working in an M2 Money state. You rely on other people to produce money for you; employees, consultants, sales and marketing people, resellers, distributors and channel partners—all contributing effort or energy in creating money for you.

In the M2 money state, you are compounding the work effort of others to produce money. Simply put: you've taken the step of cloning yourself, and if you're running your business affairs correctly, you rewarded with tax advantages. In the M2 business, *others help produce money for you on your behalf, you incur expenses which benefit both you and the business, the rest is taxed, and the balance is your salary.* In the M1 state as a W2-employee, you earn money, it's taxed, and you get to spend what's left...

For people working in an M3 Money state, real wealth creation is now taking place. People who save a part of their net income, who invest in real estate, collectibles, stocks, bonds, mutual funds, make loans to businesses, anything which creates more money from money, it's an M3 event. For most people who work as employees, the M3 level may be as far as they will go. [The exception would be Entrepreneurs who are savvy enough to "moonlight" as an Entrepreneur, while also keeping a job...]

You could debate which state is more powerful, M2 or M3. It's hard to say. Passive-income generators (M3) can create exponential growth (profit), while M2 businesses may be limited because of the market it competes in and the quality and efficiency of resources. As for complexity, they are both potentially complex. Regardless, the individual who is benefiting from the M2 and M3 state is now a true investor.

The DNA of the Master Entrepreneur (M.E.)

At the heart and soul of every "elite" or "master" entrepreneur, are the following key characteristics:

- Remains "persistent," no matter what
- Excels at intra and interpersonal communications
- Obsessed with creating value
- Thinks in "win-win" terms
- Has a personality that people are willing to work hard for
- Takes intelligent risks
- Attracts or grow leaders
- Can see value where others often can't
- Aggressively protects access to and use of, his or her time
- Has the courage to delegate important tasks to other people
- Creates ventures mainly for logical and financial reasons vs. emotional ones

Remains "persistent," no matter what

While none of the characteristics I've listed are in no particular order of importance, **without the ability to persist,** there is no way to insure or even expect success.

Let's face it: plans change, circumstances crop up; present challenges and opportunities—the unexpected (both positive and negative) simply happens.

Being persistent supports your core guidance mechanism and gives you the capacity to navigate through the choppy waters met while working your business. It's the beacon that all leaders strive to stay committed to. It's what allows you to stay true to the vision, the mission, the map and the objectives that you've decided are important enough to take action on.

It's classic: just as you commit to a direction, or a focus or action, something or someone will come along to tempt you. They will have the most incredible opportunity, or they will simply offer a better way or idea or direction to take you and your enterprise through.

There are some definite advantages to placing a single bet, having a singular focus. Often in the early phases the venture will need your undivided attention. There is real merit to doing this, but I also believe that you can, if you are careful, have more than one in play, but it comes at a cost. Your risks are much higher, as your attention is now split between endeavors. Also, your energy level must be consistently high and sufficient enough to serve them.

For me personally, I prefer having more than one venture going at a time, and I take this on only if I can create the right teams to help manage and grow them. Being an Architect Entrepreneur, I find it easy to become involved in more than one venture, but again, you have to be careful with this. You could exhaust all of your energy, only to find that in the end, nothing pans out.

So, let's say you agree with the one basket approach. You launch the business or division, and you take focused, committed actions to growing it and suddenly a "opportunity" shows up at your doorstep. It shows up in the form of a person who is the answer to your prayers, and he or she has the perfect plan to take your business to the next level. All you have to do, they say, is to steer the business in a different direction...

Well, it just so happens the current direction you've chosen has been more challenging and difficult than expected. You haven't seen the results you've planned for yet, and you are starting to feel a little burned-out and are becoming more and more disillusioned or disinterested. Wow! You say: this person or opportunity showed up just in time, and you eagerly abandon what you were doing, and steer the venture in this new (and unchartered) course . . .

At this point, you have already failed as an entrepreneur.

I hear your question: But what if the new direction turns out to be the right one? Even if it does turn out to benefit you, you've still failed, because you allowed yourself to be taken off course. By allowing yourself to go off course, you instantly placed your business squarely into harms way—you've placed it at the mercy of <u>chance</u>.

Be careful. Don't allow yourself to be seduced or enthralled by every scheme that crosses your desk. Be persistent in your commitment, your focus. If you feel your business needs a course correction, then make the correction—just make certain it is a correction and not an escape, a lure into the quick and easy world of delusion and phantom riches.

As the leader, you are your business's most powerful voice. If you are unwavering in your belief the venture is on the right path to success—then all the other investors (employees, clients, family) will believe this as well. Persist, persist, persist…

Excels at intra and interpersonal communications

The Master Entrepreneur consistently reinforces his or her actions and decisions made, through powerful and positive self-talk. When talking with themselves, they are careful in what they say to themselves. Words like *failure, loser, fraud, fool, imbecile and stupid,* are permanently missing from their dictionary.

Instead, what many see as failures become learning opportunities or become investments in their continuing education. In fact, most treat failed outcomes as valuable learning experiences, correctly realizing that, regardless of the result—an investment occurred. Ask any one of them and you will hear some version of the following: "The bottom-line is: *I committed an investment in this and I didn't get the result I was expecting. Fine. There are only two questions I now care about: What value can I take from this?* There is always value if one bothers to look for it."

This isn't just positive thinking, but instead it is an active way of controlling the quality of one's internal dialogue.

Equally important is the quality of communications with others. Entrepreneurs are careful with how they communicate with others. We hear the better they deliver their messages or directives, the higher the quality of results. Being a powerful communicator helps create wealth and potentially build critical rapport with those that work in or support the business. People are first and foremost, emotional beings. Words invoke pleasure or pain. You want to communicate in a way that gets the response and ultimately the actions that you are looking for.

The quality of your communication is directly proportional with the quality of the outcomes.
Choose your words well.

Another key ingredient to superior communication is the nonverbal communications your enterprise receives from you. Called "physiology," it represents 55% of the message. Entrepreneurs playing at this level work just as hard preserving great physiology, which is consistent with being successful, confident, competent and assured.

Communication quality is important. This is especially true for small business owners. Think about it for a moment: How do you get your employees to perform at a high-level, even though you can't fully pay them what they are worth? The currency you offer them is the promise of future reward, the present excitement of taking part in a growing business now. The currency is largely an emotionally based currency. The stronger, more compelling the communication, the greater the excitement, trust and confidence and thus the greater effort offered by them.

Small business owners are influential communicators—because they have to be. The by-product of this compensation is that owners have to spend time constantly managing people's expectations. Transacting with employees on an emotional level has a high-cost in this area. Also, it can be difficult to get employees who work based on their emotional interest or excitement, to continue to perform when things get difficult. For the small business owner, it is a classic problem: needing, but unable to pay professionals who are self-directed, results-focused and not driven emotionally.

What's the answer? There isn't any easy answer here, but it is a good idea to keep in mind that you will eventually need to transition your emotionally driven employees into different roles, as the enterprise matures. Realize that your initial core employees set the tone of the business culture and while the enterprise may need a cultural shift in the later stages of business life, employees are the lifeblood of any enterprise.

Obsessed with creating value

Much lip service is giving to the notion of *value creation, value focus, value centric*—entrepreneurs live it. The number one question that must be asked when considering the viability of an opportunity (including the enterprise) is: Does it create value? And the second: If so, for whom?

Entrepreneurs at this level worry about with *360-degree value creation*. For most, it's nearly an obsession, because they know the more value created the greater the returns. Returns in personal satisfaction, wealth, levels of success, quality of growth opportunities—everything.

Interestingly enough, when asking this group what they are doing to handle competition, most reply that they focus on innovating and competing against their previous successes. The typical reply looks like: "If my so-called competition wants to focus on what we're doing over here, more power to them. We're "a moving target," constantly evolving the enterprise. Whatever they think they are addressing nine times out of 10 will be obsolete. We're busy innovating and conditioning our customers."

Entrepreneurs who make the classic mistake of thinking that the enterprise exist to serve them find themselves struggling to win business with the best customers, have a hard time attracting and keeping the right people and staying in business long enough to squeeze out a profit. The business must be viable and stable enough to support all of its stakeholders: that's the owners, investors, employees and customers.

I have found that most weak entrepreneurs tend to think it's purely about salesmanship and pricing. "If I do a good job at constantly selling and the price is low enough, we'll get the nod." The reality is that customers *simply want their needs met or their desires answered* and they tend to buy from companies that seem to meet these needs or desires. Meeting true needs and desires trumps price. Successful entrepreneurs understand this. They also understand that a customer will pay money to meet a need or desire *they didn't even realize they had.*

Spend time now, thinking about your business concept or existing business.

- What needs does your product or service really address?
- What desires does your product or service really meet?
- What are the emotional reasons customers conduct business with you?
- Are they comforted, assured, trusting, confident-how would they describe the business relationship they have with your enterprise?
- What risk are they taking when doing business with your company versus another? What is it about your offering that allows them to be comfortable taking that risk?
- What indirect value is being created for the customer because they are doing business with you?

Knowing the answers to these questions will help you deepen your relationship with your customers and thus increase your profits. For those of you just starting out, thinking about the impact you want to have on your customers will help you assess how to market your business, tailor your product or service offering and give you more confidence that you'll create real value for them and thus deserve having the sale.

Why the obsession over value? Because you want to eliminate any doubt you might have that your company deserves the business it wins. Customers *hate* dealing with companies that are not confident in their offering. Remember, your transactions with your external and internal customers (employees) are largely emotional. Master

Entrepreneurs understand this and drive their business from this understanding.

Whoa...what's this about deserving the business that I've won? You want to avoid the roller coaster of having to "pull it off." Often, winning business is easier than fulfilling the commitment that is created with having won the business. You want to avoid having that hollow feeling which comes from getting business based on false claims, stretched truths and impossible assurances.

While you might "pull it off," it won't feel good. And yes, it's revenue, but like a gambler on a lucky streak, you will one day find yourself giving it all back—through mistakes, bills, spending sprees. Don't laugh: I've seen it happen. Earn your winnings; build wealth that you are deserving of and that befits your good character. No shortcuts—serve your customers well and they'll reward you justly...

Is "win-win" oriented

So, I just lost some of you with this statement, right? Let's be clear: an entrepreneur can generate wealth with a win-lose mindset. Yep, it happens everyday. Kill or be killed, let the best man win, etc. Heard them all.

I'm talking about entrepreneurs desiring to excel and create *outrageous* wealth. To do this requires a win-win mindset. Wealth is cumulative and flows to those who best utilize it. Also, wealth creation is reciprocal in nature: the more value you create for others, the more energy you and your enterprise expend, the greater the return. It has been said that the universe "abhors a vacuum." If one believes this, then whatever energy or contribution you create for the world, that energy must be replaced (returned).

Do you really want to be the guy who struggles to list the friends and colleagues that admire you, but who can rapidly name a long list of enemies?

Does the notion of creating a business filled with aggressive "I'm in it for myself" employees, who execute out of fear vs. respect really excite you?

Does having equally ruthless customers, who are always angling for leverage over you (crazy, creeping projects, vague financial commitments, hazy contracts) really get your juices flowing?

If so, I say Wow, more power to you. Don't read any further. This book can't do a thing for you.
For the rest of you, let's keep going, shall we?

Win-win is what it's all about. You're demanding, but fair with your workers (who reward you with allegiance and their best efforts), you tell the truth to your customers (who reward this with bankable business), to business partners who work with you versus secretly angling against you. It feels good, it's good for you and it's good for the greater good. Why would you do anything else?

The win-win mindset is the right thing to do, it's rarely done and its a really powerful level to operate from. I believe that only 10% of the world's top enterprises operate at this level—and all dominate their industries.

Okay, so what's in it for you, the Master Entrepreneur in the making? Happier workers, relieved and pleasantly surprised customers and happier spouses, better restful nights sleep—need we go on? I've done the math on this one—it equates to success and profit 100% of the time.

Has a personality that people are willing to work hard for

Personality, charisma, strength of character... The M.E. has the kind of personality that people will "walk through fire" for. They are aware of the effect they have on their staff and actively seek to set the tone for the way business is run. Entrepreneurs with the strongest charisma have employees emulate their mannerisms, attitudes and beliefs. For example, in strategy meetings, Bill Gates, Chairman of Microsoft, would end up hunched over in his chair, rocking back in forth while considering what he was hearing.

This mannerism is well-known and immediately was emulated by many of Microsoft's top executives and managers. The bottom line is strong leaders impact their peers and subordinates on both a conscious and unconscious level. The enlightened leader will make use of this tendency, by instilling the thinking and behaviors desired for the company's culture.

Takes intelligent risks

Intelligent risk. What's that mean? It means that an action is taken after all reasonable factors have been considered and despite having incomplete information. Entrepreneurs from all walks of life are famous for taking actions; actions that were previously thought impossible. The fact is, we don't know what we don't know — this is both a blessing and a curse. Entrepreneurs regularly have to take whatever information's available and commit to a decision. Working with less than perfect information is as natural as breathing to an entrepreneur.

Still, the M.E. carefully considers the impact, the results of an action. He or she tries to assess the total risk of taking on (or not) that potential contract, customer, partner and employee. They look at the impact on culture, cash flow, direction, focus, energy — everything.

Entrepreneurs who don't carefully consider the risk can quickly find themselves taken out of the game. Case in point: with 8(a) firms (small minority-owned businesses) it is not uncommon for these firms to be "cash strapped." A typical 8(a) firm has most of their revenues coming from the government sector.

They often tap credit lines to cover payroll and other overhead expenses, as they wait for payment from the government. Meanwhile, they constantly strive to win new 8(a) contracts. Often, they spend all of their time focusing on submitting and winning the contract and fail to consider the cash needed to carry out the contract before receiving payment. I've heard many horror stories of essentially profitable firms sunk because they failed to consider the impact on cash flow that piece of won business would have on the company. So they fail because there's not enough cash to cover the overhead. A horrible reason for failure, don't you think?

Number one rule: Grow and protect your cash flow. Cash is the oxygen of any enterprise—if there is no cash, there is no business.

Risks come in big and small packages. A big risk, typical of growing small business, occurs when considering office moves and leases. A typical example might go like this: your existing business is in a tight, but acceptable office space. The lease payment is made comfortably every month. Meanwhile, you've had a string of "wins." A couple of company-sponsored lunches later, a new hire or two later, a question is posed. Should we consider moving to a larger office? We have the revenues to support it and we are obviously growing—what do we think?

The master entrepreneur and those key leaders around him or her should all see red flags. The immediate questions are:

Does the string of won business really reflect a shift in the company's market, or did we just have a great quarter?

Are we growing, or are we simply looking to buy a "trophy," marking the occasion?

Does moving to a new location create real value to the company, meaning will we be more efficient, productive?

Does it increase value to our existing customers?

Often, entrepreneurs fall into the trap of expanding too quickly, against phantom revenue growth and to gain a physical trophy, marking a significant moment of success. Please, please—please resist doing this. It's the same as buying too much house or too much car. All of a sudden, you are working for the bank and all your profits are paid to the past, instead of invested forward. Learn to be aggressive in protecting the company's cash. You worked hard for it—protect it from leaking away.

Those copiers, computer, fax machine, employee—all of these are investments. Investments made against cash or revenues; investments that must net more than they cost.

Leases lock you in. They are nearly impossible to break without taking a financial hit, can slow you down when you need to streamline material overhead, or even reposition the company, say out-of-state. Equipment bought outright can travel quickly with you and are sold just as quickly. Leases are not liquid and don't travel. Be careful.

Please understand, I know how tough it can be, launching and growing a business and the unexpected sacrifices you might incur. It's natural to want to celebrate that first big win. It feels so good to have finally made a breakthrough, profit, landing the deal... Celebrate by continuing to carry out your plan.

Attracts or grow leaders

The master entrepreneur has their eye on the prize—the door marked exit. We will discuss the exit in detail later, but because of this focus, entrepreneurs playing at this level, begin the enterprise searching for potential leaders. Of all the investments an M.E. must think about for the enterprise, this is the most essential.

In the beginning, the typical entrepreneur must do everything and wear many hats. But eventually, business growth will demand that the entrepreneur shift roles and responsibilities down and throughout the enterprise. Leaders must be acquired, or developed. "I need to replicate myself" is the typical comment from many entrepreneurs.

Now were getting to it. It's the toughest thing in the world to entrust one's child to another. It's the same for business owners. They have to have enough courage to delegate key responsibilities to others. It's a tough: there are so many seemingly great excuses for not going through with it:

"They are just going to mess it up and I'll have to step in again and..."

"It's too complicated—I'm stuck with it..."

"I don't think he (she) is up to the challenge. What if he or she..."

And on and on. Find a way. Do it anyway. The longer you hang on to all those identities or roles—the more money you are losing the company. If you persist in doing it all yourself—take on a job and close up shop. You'll make just as much money in the end. Don't believe it? Believe it. Yes, your company will make a lot of money—a lot of it—maybe, but the net income to you personally will not be there. Here's what it looks like:

Since you're doing everything yourself, YOU are the main factor driving sales. Truly, you've just created a job, a M1 money event, except now you are paying salaries and office lease payments and what not, so you are sharing your M1 income with the entire enterprise! Is this what you signed on for? Of course not.

When operating in this state, if you shut down or decide to take a vacation, the entire enterprise comes to a screeching halt. Just check the number of emails, pages and voicemails next time if you don't believe that…

Customers are never properly conditioned to see a company. Why should they? It's you who shows up at all hours, saving the day, resolving a "crisis."

Sound familiar? I seriously hope not. Identify the potential leaders in your company and develop them. Get it done; it's the least risky action you can take that benefits both you and your company.

Can see value where others often can't

Seek to aim for investments with the highest value. Go after the best customer, hire great people, develop the most profitable products and services at the right time and spend your time for maximum return. It seems elementary, but many companies just don't do this. Spend your time making great investments—make it a habit to figure out the profit on everything. Be aggressive, be conservative, either way, just do the assessment and take action with a sense of profit in mind.

By now, you should be noticing a pattern: every action, every decision, every thought or plan or consideration or hire is an "investment." Energy, commitment, motivation, emotions, money, service, customers—all are investments. All of them. Master Entrepreneurs are always assessing values and returns.

For them, it's an automatic thing--they can't help themselves. It's a habit engrained at the DNA level. Get in the habit of seeing everything as an investment. Your employees, your time, company mission, its identity, its customers, products and services, cash, expenses—all are investments.

Aggressively protects access to and use of, his or her time

A common example of this needing to occur is when an entrepreneur suddenly finds themselves fighting to protect their time. Where once, everyone had access to the owner all the time, now the owner is faced with running a large company. He or She needs to conserve their energy and focus on important and valuable activities.

Suddenly, voicemails are no longer quickly returned, e-mail is unread, meetings often canceled. If you have a company filled with "A" players, who are self-directed and operate from internal motivation and not emotion—you will have no problem. In fact, most will be thinking, "It's about time." If your organization is filled with "B" players, who are emotionally motivated, most will misinterpret your actions and many will take it as a personal slight.

To avoid this, you will need to prepare the workforce in advance—let them know it's coming and that it isn't personal. Better still, have your management team handle it. Shift the initial contact/access through them; make it official and your team will be okay with it.

> Energy, Focus, Time and Money:
> *The four key elements*
> *to investment success.*
> You have to protect them *all.*

Creates ventures mainly for logical and financial reasons vs. emotional ones

Being in business for the right reasons. Of course it's okay to start a business because you are excited. On some level, there must be some emotion propelling you through the fear and uncertainty to actually do it—to create the business. But there should also be other reasons, sound, practical, logical reasons for starting the business as well.

You see a need or desire that's not fulfilled by others and you think you can create a company that addresses it. You think there is a real opportunity to make enough money at something to justify creating a business and you think you have enough resources to benefit from it. Starting a business to prove something to someone is just not a good enough reason. In fact, if it's purely for emotional reasons—it can be a costly experience.

There are enough real threats and issues to address in growing an enterprise than to go into one fighting ghosts.

The ghosts of others ridicule, you know; ridicule like "You're a dreamer, you'll never succeed in business. Be practical. Get a good job," and other such disempowering things. Sure, you can start a business, fueled by anger, by bruised ego, shaken identity—but eventually you'll need other resources to sustain your efforts and effectively grow the business in the right way.

Going into a business on pure emotion harms the chances of the business surviving. Why? Because: it's about the founder-not the enterprise. Not even it's customers. It's about the owner. Meanwhile, employees hop on, customers risk doing business, investors pony up some capital—all thinking they are investing in a viable business, when in fact it isn't a business at all. It's the owners' shell of himself/herself. The U.S. statistic of annual business failures will never be accurate, because many of those businesses were just high-paying jobs.

Go into this for the right reasons. If ever there was a time to be honest with yourself, it's in that moment before you turn the ignition. Be sure: it's the most responsible and powerful thing you can do in that moment.

In talking with several successful entrepreneurs, I found that many had to endure some degree of negative feedback-and the most common group to provide this was from friends and relatives. It's interesting-- people, who have never even run a business or even thought about doing so, are the ones who enthusiastically offer "words of wisdom" and caution. They are also the ones most likely to talk about how much luck or money or other thing is required and that of course you probably don't have these to succeed. In the end, they will wish you well.

As an author and entrepreneur I can attest to this. I have had to avoid the "good intentions" of family and friends and just do the business anyway. Don't be surprised if you find yourself having to do the same. While friends and family may have your best interest at heart, their support is harmful to you. Seek guidance and support from people who have accomplished what you are striving for.

There are several ways you can make certain you're headed in the right direction concept-wise. You can seek out others who have either done similar businesses or are in the same industry you're planning to play in. Or, you can seek those who have relevant experience starting and running a business. I encourage all entrepreneurs new and old alike, to create their personal "Board of Advisers."

Sometimes having someone with your best interest at heart, who isn't "in the soup" can save you. Having a trusted source on the outside, with a birds' eye view of your business can often lead to valuable suggestions and observations that wouldn't normally have occurred. When I set out to write this book, I first set up a small advisory team to help me stay on track to produce the book I wanted to create.

To do this, I shared with them what my goals were for the book, who I thought the readers would be and explained the experience and value I wanted the reader to have. I told them what my "rules" were; what I did and did not want the book to convey, the directions I wanted to take the book in and the needs I was committed to addressing.

Being entrepreneurs themselves, they were happy to help, but boy, they were tough! I hope the result is that you find this book to be fantastic read.

Having a personal advisory team is powerful. You benefit from their collective brainpower and it can be a means of great power and confidence, knowing that strong people are behind you, routing you on.

I also strongly suggest that you open yourself up to becoming an adviser for at least one other businessperson. For one, it feels good to help someone; for another it helps sharpen your skills and deepen your knowledge of business.

CHAPTER TWO
The Four Entrepreneurial Types

"I walked for miles at night along the beach, composing bad blank verse and searching endlessly for someone wonderful who would step out of the darkness and change my life. It never crossed my mind that that person could be me."
-Anna Quindlen

There are four distinct types of Entrepreneurs:
Architects
Builders
Managers
Integrators

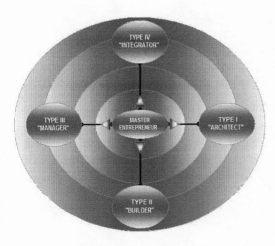

In any successful, growing enterprise, there can be found one of the four types. All are important and necessary. No one type is greater than the other. In fact, most have to work in harmony effectively contributing their abilities to the mission.

As I mentioned earlier, many individuals, especially the cash-strapped small business startup entrepreneur, find themselves having to play all of these roles. However, at some point (usually sooner rather than later), people who excel in one of these categories must be involved.

By understanding the various types, you have a unique opportunity; you have the opportunity to create a business team or gain partners with the right entrepreneurial skill at the right time.

For example, you might seek support of a person who excels at planning and strategy (Architect) and have yet another person (perhaps yourself), carry out the plan (Builder). Once the business is off life-support and is stable, you bring in another entrepreneurial-type person to manage the result (Manager). And when your enterprise arrives at maturity and the exit is near, you then bring in a seasoned Architect, Builder or Manager and merge it or explode its growth through a well-timed acquisition...

Here is a graphical summary of the entrepreneurial types needed based on the business cycle. This model will be discussed in detail later in the enterprise section of the book but for now, just make note of the natural alignment:

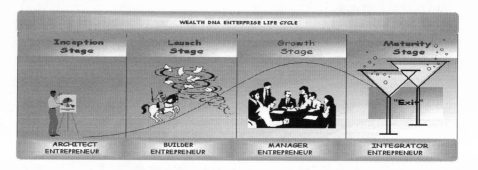

Type I Entrepreneurs: "The Architects"

Type I Entrepreneurs excel at creating the planning and strategy around business development. They come up with the ideas and test it against existing opportunities. They give thought to the resources that will be needed and they set a plan of action. Being natural researchers, they explore all of the details needed for the setup. They look at the business structure, figuring out the local, state and federal laws that might apply against the business, and the capital required to launch it. They set the "tone" of the idea, create the vision and establish the ideal customer profiles. And finally, they predict the types of systems (accounting, legal, administration, sales, marketing, etc.) necessary to launch the business.

The mind and their imagination are their primary playing ground, and Architects excel at seeing and planning towards the future. In fact, they can see several futures. They have a tendency to be addicted to growth and learning, and often display keen interest in various subject matters.

One of the interesting things about entrepreneurs in this group is their ability to juxtapose ideas from unrelated areas and combine them in a way that results in a new way. The weakest in the group live their entire lives "in their head." The futures that they see and the richness of their imagination often is more compelling than addressing the real world.

If a person with architect tendencies isn't entrepreneuring or intrapreneuring, they can often be found multi-tasking as a major line resource, producing incredible amounts of output for the organization they work in. The challenge with this is, the process they've designed to produce this work is so complex, that it isn't easily replicated, so if this person leaves the organization—the ability to produce this output walks out with them.

Architects love designing strategies and systems and are often more interested in this than the results these things produce. The strongest in this realm care about both, and can work envisioning the future while at the same time acknowledging present conditions (reality).

I hear a lot of saying to yourselves: "Man! I've got an architect working for me. How do I manage them?" The answer: it's tricky trying to manage architects. Architects are the odd birds in the entrepreneur family: they love designing systems and structures for others to run in, but they detest having to operate the structures themselves.

The solution is don't try to manage them. Instead, *lead them with intelligence.* Put your best and brightest people on their case. Architects admire beauty and intellect. Steer them to action using logic and reason, not threats. In fact, it's often best if you just state the objective, and let them figure out the solution to get there. It's tough dealing with Architects, because you can't influence them with threats, with money, like you can with other employees. These people are completely confident that they can design solutions to their problems, and tend to be driven by intellectual interest in the project/job/opportunity than the financial reward, so to appeal to them, you have to appeal to their mind, their mental interest.

If you need Architects to play on a team, place them on a team with the most difficult, riskiest, complex objectives. The men and women that play Architect are the intellectual thoroughbreds of the group—their strength is strength of mind. You can often find these people playing in the consultant arena, putting out fires and helping others prevent fires. The best of them strike a balance between *what they see* in terms of a client's future, and *what that client is ready to hear.*

> The key to being a great Architect is to balance the beauty of tomorrow with the needs of today.

A lot of entrepreneurs fail to give enough (if any) thought and time here. Instead, they just launch, assuming that there will be time later to address certain issues. Sometimes, they are right, but often it proves very expensive for the business later. Good business architecture helps insure the right foundation and initial systems are in place to build and grow from.

While the upfront costs are high (money, time, risk to momentum and the excitement of the concept), the future payoff is enormous. It takes a person with good discipline and courage to set the guidelines and the rules of play, while resisting the urge to just go for it. Architects establish the basic blueprint of the enterprise, from which others can intelligently build upon. Would you build a house without blueprints? Of course not. But surprisingly, many entrepreneurs fail to see the importance of the planning stage.

The Benefits of being a Type I (Architect) Entrepreneur:

- There are no shortages of business concepts needing this essential skill
- Business concepts involving architectural types early have the highest probability of achieving *sustainable* success
- Being this type assures the involvement of others, therefore delegation and the presence of a business team is guaranteed- so the threat of creating a job out of the venture becomes greatly diminished.

The Risks of being a Type I Entrepreneur:

- Without the right mix of entrepreneurs present, there is a tendency to over-plan and under-execute. So instead of "Ready, aim—Fire!" you have: "Ready? Aim, aim, aim…"

- There are practically zero roles to play in a mature, "status-quo" business; most contributions are made in the startup, growth and/or recovery stages of the enterprise.

- Success of the venture isn't controlled by the architect, only influenced; other entrepreneurs are required to cultivate the business, so there is a heavy reliance on others.

- Weak architect types can design too much complexity in the enterprise too soon. This potentially threatens the viability of the business and puts this entrepreneur's credibility with others at risk. Margins for error are very slim here. *(The key is to constantly educate the other parties involved and to steer your designs toward simplicity vs. complexity. Keep it real and keep it grounded enough in the present. Try not to incorporate too much future planning.)*

Being an Architect type myself, I can't emphasize enough how important it is that you generate strategies based on present business conditions. As you will see in later discussion, it is paramount that the Builder type both understand and believe in the strategies you design. For him or her to do so, it must be relevant enough to address current issues and opportunities.

If your planning is too complex, or based on events too far forward into the future, you will not have the buy-in necessary from the other entrepreneurial types. They will simply ignore the plan and thus assume higher risks than is called for. In my case, my partner at Swift 1 Financial was a builder entrepreneur, one who trusts his "inner circle," so I was able to design powerful strategies, while simultaneously gaining feedback from them.

For those of you that don't have this luxury, keep in mind the following adage: Less is truly more. Keep it real and keep it simple.

The best in this group are great at seeing patterns, seeing sequences of possibility and actions. They are very good at identifying resources and maximizing the use of these resources through carefully planning. Of the four, Architects are the deep thinkers and can see the running of the enterprise well in advance of launch. While architects relate closest to the Integrator type, the success or failure of their planning and strategies rest squarely on their shoulders of the Builder types.

The strong Builder type recognizes the value Architects can bring in terms of charting the course. Less experienced Builders tend to ignore or undervalue the Architect's role—often to their folly.

"Getting ahead in a difficult profession requires avid faith in yourself. You must be able to sustain yourself against staggering blows. That is why some people with mediocre talent, but with great inner drive, go much farther than people with vastly superior talent."

~ Sophia Loren

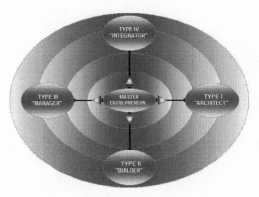

Type II Entrepreneurs: "The Builders"

Ah, the real trailblazers of the bunch...

Type II Entrepreneurs assemble the resources, create the identity, activate the plan and processes and spend capital. While Architects conceptualize and establish the *framework* for the enterprise, Builders initiate the actual *creation* of the enterprise. Examples of Type II Entrepreneurs-- there are many since this type represents the largest pool of entrepreneurs by population. Howard Hughes, John D. Rockefeller Sr., Sam Walton of Wal-Mart fame, Aristotle Onassis, Henry Ford Sr., Donald Trump and the list goes on and on. When the media reports on the activities of a company, 9 times out of 10, you'll find the Type II front and center.

Builders are like surfers seeking the perfect wave—they seek momentum wherever they can find it, using it like a surfer uses wave formation to setup their run, Builders use momentum to generate and feed excitement. They thrive working in the blind and they are the type most comfortable operating under uncertain environments. For them, the payoff is in the action. The wisest Type II's respect the presence of a good plan (usually) and use it to good advantage (if they trust it).

Really, it's all about the action *and the results*. In general, subordinates, employees, non-manager types love being lead by Builder energy. "It's crazy around here, but damn, where else can you go to get this much excitement?" Weak Type II's burnout resources; they work hard, they play harder, and run until they shut down. Most of the businesses that fail, fail because they were run purely on Builder-type energy. Growth, getting the sale, succeeding at all cost were the mantras of these failed businesses and often these were the sole priority or focus.

When one of my partners started his first company ten years ago, man it was exciting, but they were all over the place. He found himself taking advice from all kinds of people (and no, they didn't have the benefit of an Architect at the time). Back then, they created a company based on his belief that the product was incredible and because it was so incredible—customers would see that and simply buy, buy, buy. Well, they were half-right.

They operated from the belief that a great idea would be rewarded with profit, when they should have realized that great businesses are rewarded. They were so caught up in the excitement of what they were doing, that they never got around to the hard stuff, those boring things like, cost projections, revenue projections, marketing campaigns, team building.

Fortunately, they were able to evolve the company, and turn it into a very successful endeavor. Truly, Builders are the warrior-class, but even Kings seek the council and headed the wisdom of the wizard ("Architect"). Learn to trust the power of planning and strategy and train yourself to be addicted to results and not just the "action." Without exception, every business concept must have a Type II entrepreneur in its lifetime.

The Benefits of being a Type II (Builder) Entrepreneur:

- Masters at exploiting and responding to fast developing opportunities.
- People are naturally attracted to the Type II's energy. Motivating resources to action is easy for this type.
- Strong ability to take actions/risks, despite not having complete information. Will work "in the dark," if that's what it takes.
- Excel at working under crisis and urgency. Quick decision making ability. Not shy in taking responsibility.
- Can easily shift focus and direction of the enterprise when situations call for this.

The Risks of being a Type II Entrepreneur:

- Operating without the right planning and strategy, there is a tendency to over-react to opportunities, any opportunities. "Ready? fire! fire! fire!..."
- Can easily become addicted to the action, to the crisis's faced by the enterprise
- High tendency for burn-out of self and others
- Tend to delegate critical functions away to others
- Tendency to push the enterprise to constant innovation for innovation's sake
- Tend to be possessive of the enterprise, often seeing the enterprise as an "extension" or mirror of themselves

If you are a Type II Entrepreneur, watch for signs of addiction. All businesses eventually "mature," recognize this when it happens and train yourself to be okay with it.

Training companies like Envision U run into Type II's more than any other group. They hear how their companies are meeting their numbers, maintaining the status quo and how distressing it is for them. "I woke up one morning and found we had 50 employees, all working in accounting and other back-office functions. Found myself asking: What exactly do they do? What impact are they having to the bottom line?"

When Envision U assesses the company, often it will find no significant problems—every function is executing as needed. But what it does find is a bored Type II, anxious to take on something-anything. The challenge is that the Type II "Builder" now finds themselves in an administrator capacity and they're itching to create or respond to something. Type II's are the first volunteers to develop that new business unit or cost center—anything involving action, challenge and potential crisis. They are like surfers, looking for the next big wave to ride.

The best in this group temper their need for action and momentum, with the wisdom and patience of taking the time to build systems. Builders who mature, who survive or avoid burnout from over-extending themselves and their energy, learn to pace themselves. They value the advantage of having great plans and strategies to execute from and they have learned to appreciate people who are driven to organize, manage and follow through. Yes, they still yearn for the rush of racing on the edge, but they realize that it's not only important to show up and play, but to have enough left over to finish and win.

Builders who understand the power in developing and leading great teams are often wildly successful, both in business and in their personal lives. They attract the right people, performing in the right roles at the right time. This gives them the freedom to live a full life while building on the enterprise.

One of my ex-partners (a Builder) was an avid golfer and fan of golf. I remember having a conversation with him one day about this very topic: living a full life. Once, while playing golf with a few business associates, one of them took to my partner immediately. They quickly struck up a conversation, discussing business—my partner's startup and the associate's 10-year old business.

This gentleman shared something very important to my partner that day. He told him that he designed his business to operate without him, without requiring his daily oversight into the minutia of day-to-day details. At this point, he only goes into the office twice a week, mainly to meet with key clients and to be debriefed by his executive team.

My partner then spent the next hour or so, asking about and learning this gentleman's strategies for creating this organization. He was impressed and so was I. It hadn't even dawned on us this would even be possible or desired. And we have now applied a lot of the strategies learned that day into our exit strategy for the business.

Builders are the warrior-class of entrepreneur; they are best in the face of battle.

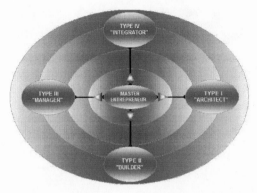

Type III Entrepreneurs: "The Managers"

The business model is perfected. The enterprise has staked out a hefty chunk of its market, the right employees are in place, doing the right things and because of the culture you've created, *thinking the right way.* Investors are more relaxed now, because the storms have past and they can see the "port over the bow" (the exit). Ah, Life is good...

At this point, Type III Entrepreneurs are running the show. They are the specialist-administrator, presiding, watching and monitoring the "vital signs" of the business. Protecting the status quo, seeking consistency everywhere. Consistent revenues, predictable execution, steady overhead levels. If you had to navigate a large boat through iceberg-laden oceans, the Type III manager is your go-to guy, hands down. Some well known Type III's include: Sam Walsh of Wal-Mart and Meg Whitman of eBay and Alan Greenspan, Chairman of the Federal Reserve.

Where employees may or may not like Type II's, they respect Type III's. Employees at this stage of the venture are not addicted to the action or fueled by excitement. Instead, they execute based on the comfort of knowing that tomorrow will look very similar to today and the next day to the day before. Nearly everyone in the business will be interested in familiarity and routine. The original founders of the business are long gone, or are only remotely involved with the business. They are likely off building on another venture. If they are involved, it's only to see the company positioned for the exit.

And in terms of the exit: if, for example, the exit is either an initial public offering or simply a private sale, it is very likely that the Type III Entrepreneur will continue with the company, even after the acquisition.

I can think of no more important phase than when the enterprise has just reached its mature state. Often, a business can be sold during the growth phase, but the "real money" is when the business has just entered the calm waters that maturity brings. Owners, early stakeholders finally know exactly what kind of a winner they have on their hands. Potential buyers, while having to pay maximum price, are at least comforted in knowing that they are faced with purchasing a real and viable business, vs. a concept or flash in the pan. The value of the exit during this stage is at the highest level, because the business is thriving, not surviving. While no one can predict the future, the present is very profitable indeed...

Type III's are the natural custodians of a business that, by its continued existence, has earned both the
right to exist and to continue operating. They work with the CIO or CFO of the acquiring company to plot out the transition strategy and Type III's serve as a beacon for the resources being acquired. This is the ideal scenario.

A lot of mergers & acquisitions (M&A) were done in such a poor way; the acquirer purchases the firm and fires the entire management team, falsely assuming integration simply wouldn't require it. Now, companies involved with M&A actions are a lot smarter, the most successful acquiring a company and leaving it largely in tact.

If we look to Warren Buffet's strategy, we find that Warren eliminates the bulk of this risk, by focusing on acquiring the business based upon its leadership team. For him, the quality of a company's leadership holds the bulk of the company's intrinsic value…

The Benefits of being a Type III (Manager) Entrepreneur:
- Excels at administration and maintaining the status quo of the mature enterprise. They find reward in consistent performance, vs. constant growth.
- Completely comfortable managing a large and complex organization.
- Tendency to be very results-focused and customer-oriented. Customer's satisfaction and overall experience with the company at this stage is both high and predictable.
- Tendency to excel in a liaison capacity, between original founders/owners, investors and potential suitors (seeking to acquire the firm).

The Risks of being a Type III Entrepreneur:
- Can be slow to respond to sudden, unexpected crisis.
- Tend to be resistant to innovation-related projects.
- Are not always quick to abandon outdated processes.
- Tend to be slow to respond to new business opportunities.

- Slow to hire, slow to fire—sometimes resulting in loss of candidates, or higher operating cost due to performance issues.

Perhaps the #1 complaint directed at Type III's is that they are sometimes seen as too rigid in their thinking. Creative types, sales and marketing folks—while they enjoy getting paid on time, but find it difficult to present a new concept. Type III's are by their nature too structured to accommodate these needs and desires well. The organization would do well to bring in the Type I's and II's to plan and execute the strategy while the Type III manages the hands that feed them all.

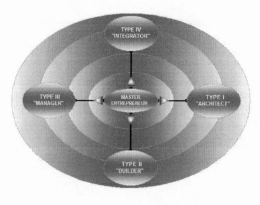

Type IV Entrepreneurs: "The Integrators"

Type IV Integrator entrepreneurs are an interesting breed. Some famous ones you may know are, Bill Gates, Warren Buffet, Sandy Weill, T. Boone Pickens, Andrew Carnegie, Ted Turner and Oprah Winfrey. Entrepreneurs playing at this level are seeking to either build empires or manage the ones they have created-and they have the means to do so. Type IV Entrepreneurs come to being as a result of previous entrepreneurial successes they've had, while being in the role of any of the first three types.

Often, integration comes from the necessity of managing the aftermath of a string of successes. Oprah Winfrey's enterprise, Harpo Productions, Inc. was so successful in every media product it produced, it resulted in the creation of: O Magazine, Oprah After the Show, Oprah's Book Club, The Angel Network and their latest media hit "The Dr. Phil Show." Within a span of a few years, Oprah went from a respected talk-show host to a full-fledged media mogul, managing over a dozen different products and companies.

Warren Buffet, Chairman of Berkshire Hathaway, Inc. is probably the best example of a Type IV Entrepreneur in modern times.

Pouring through their most recent annual report, one finds that the Hathaway conglomeration has fifty-eight distinct businesses, ranging from a candy manufacturer and a kitchen accessories business to an underwear company (Fruit of the Loom). Berkshire's businesses throw off so much cash, that it necessitates Warren Buffet and Charlie Munger to be on the constant lookout for acquisitions. What's really interesting is Warren's focus on the leaders, the managers of the various enterprises.

Throughout the Chairman's 21-page letter, are many, many references to the specific achievements of various Presidents, V.P.'s and other key executive managers. Entrepreneurs take note—The Berkshire business model is textbook, best-in-class.

If you have ever wondered what it will be like when one day you are in charge of a large business, your business—read some of Warren and Charlie's letters. They talk about momentum, risks, errors in strategy and decisions that they've made, strategies to correct, the reasons for acquiring the businesses they acquired — the whole gamut of areas of focus and day-to-day, quarter-by-quarter concerns typical of all business owners. It is highly recommended reading.

A lot of entrepreneurs simply have no desire to grow their enterprise to such a level that acquisitions are the necessary "next step." For these entrepreneurs, the exit will have already occurred, typically at the first merger or by some other transition.

Speaking of mergers, another great example of a Type IV integrator (Intrapreneur in this case) is Larry Kinder of Cendant Corporation. As CIO of this multi-billion dollar conglomeration, Larry and his management team are responsible for successfully merging entire companies into the Cendant infrastructure.

Envision U, was fortunate in helping him map out some of the key communication strategies to assist with rapidly aligning and integrating the management teams of the acquired companies. Because Larry's approach is so systematized, he has been able to achieve extraordinary results, previously not achieved in Cendant's history.

The Benefits of being a Type IV (Integrator) Entrepreneur:
- The enterprise is rich in capital resources & other means of leverage to acquire companies outright

- The majority of decisions made by Type IV have a global impact on the business and its revenues; often, an immediate impact

- The role involves strategy, planning, execution, risk and management skills to handle the after-math of an acquisition, thus being of interest of all three entrepreneurial types

- As a result of a successful acquisition, a tremendous amount of value creation is created for all customers (employees, owners, creditors, customers) due to increased diversity of product or service offering

The Risks of being a Type IV Entrepreneur:
Most of the common risks for an entrepreneur playing at this level are basically decision-outcome related. Buying the right business for the wrong price; failure to consider a key condition or factor; poor discipline and thus execution for unloading bad bets.

Possibly the worst is walking into a situation with too much confidence (where EGO is driving the deal). Case in point: the AOL Time-Warner merger. Others include:

- Pursing the wrong acquisition (or just simply getting it wrong) can potential sink the ship*

- Miscalculating the short-term and possibly long-term *negative* impact on existing revenues an acquisition might have.

- Inadvertently taking on too much growth too quickly through acquisition, assuming previous past successful acquisitions predict future successes.

- Miscalculating the expected benefits (increased cash flows, profit, organizational efficiency, "synergies") of a potential acquisition.

Even the best of the best sometimes get it wrong. Taking Warren Buffet as an example; he readily admits that acquiring the company Berkshire-Hathaway, getting into the textiles business, was perhaps the worst business decision he's made in recent memory. His best: Geico. In both cases, the aftermath/impact both made on his core businesses were profound and more to the point, unanticipated.

CHAPTER III
The DNA of the Superior Enterprise

*"Find a game worth playing.
Play as if your life &
sanity depends upon it.
If life doesn't seem to offer
a game worth playing,
Then Invent One.
Any Game is Better than No Game"- Unknown*

No matter whether we are a Type I or IV, we are all in it to grow something, to build something great. Growing a business is like creating a new game. It requires passion, curiosity, imagination and emotional commitment to bring it to life. All growth stems from the mindset of a company's leadership. Of all those responsible for creating and encouraging growth, Entrepreneurs are the true "mad scientist" of the business community. I'd like to think that the world couldn't run without us! Give us the dice, we say, we'll roll it to victory!

I believe it's every great entrepreneur's dream to build an outstanding company. A company filled with great people, doing great things for great customers. It's the payoff at the end of the day. Having a great company in the end makes all the risks, sacrifices and hard work meaningful. What does a great company or superior enterprise look like? Regardless of size, all great companies have the following key attributes:

- It is powered by systems vs. the efforts of an individual
- It attracts and retains "A" players found throughout the organization
- It has very profitable and deep customer base
- It has the right resources deployed in the right way at the right time
- It is designed to be very cash flow efficient
- It is a business which can grow and be grown for the right reasons
- It provides distinct value for its customers, at an advantage over other competitors
- It is a business focused on creating value through innovation
- It competes in the marketplace as a proactive business vs. reactive business
- It is a business which rewards all stakeholders

Some of you may be saying to yourself "That's great. But I'm just starting my business. How is this relevant to me?" It's very relevant, especially for those of you just starting out. Imagine being able to see the future *before it happens,* seeing the results of shortcuts taken, knowing in advance the impact of taking on the wrong customer—all before you even open your doors? By creating a business that reflects these attributes, you save time, money and increase your odds of seeing the business succeed. Let's take a closer look, shall we?

It is powered by systems vs. the efforts of an individual

A **system**, in this case, is: *anything which provides a framework for executing and achieving results on a consistent and predictable basis.*

Some of you reading this already know the power in having great systems in place—payroll, contract/proposal development, hiring processes, sales process, etc. The best companies have systems for everything: from preset formats to use for letter and email generation, rules governing when to call a meeting, who should attend and how it should be conducted, to handling inquiries about the company. They realize that systems provide the best opportunity to generate consistent performance and outcomes over time.

If you were to ask me, what is the most important thing an entrepreneur can do, I'd have to say that creating systems for your business to operate in is probably the most important activity you can do for your business. I can feel some of you shaking your heads on this. You're thinking that getting cash flow into the business is the most important, right? Well, cash flow is the *life blood* of the enterprise, and it's really, really important, but it's the systems that are the real predictors of success, of even being able to sustain that hard won cash.

I've made a lot of people upset with me when I tell them that their systems are more important than the contract they just landed. Somehow, they feel as though maybe I've misunderstood them, that I somehow don't really appreciate the success that landing that piece of business brings them. I understand. I understand that if they don't have good systems in place on the backend, it will be next to impossible for them to realize full profit from that hard one piece of business.

Business owners that operate from focusing only on the cash, find that they need to bring in more and more of it just to keep the lights on. They know that they should implement that payroll system or hire a payroll service. They know that they owe their accountant some quality time so that this accountant can accurately setup their books. They know that they should put in some time and create sales scripts and talking point documents for the newly hired sales rep— they know all of this yet things are just too urgent right now.

You tell yourself that it will have to wait. Meanwhile, you've hired people, you've hired consultants like an accountant to provide your business things—and by not focusing on creating the systems, you've placed the entire business at risk.

In this scenario, the only winners are the creditors, and maybe the bank. Employees are hurt, investors (read: customers) are burned, and dreams are destroyed.

A word of advice: never get so busy that you neglect creating the systems needed to support and run your business. It is at least as important as generating cash flow, and in many cases, its more important. Entrepreneurs who make it a habit of building systems for everything tend to be able to recognize the wealth that already surrounds them.

To build a "system," means you've created a process of doing something, one that consistently delivers results, and that's worth repeating over and over again. Systems-oriented entrepreneurs are easily identified; they are the ones constantly asking: "Can this be repeated?" "How can we replicate this process?" "Is there a better/cheaper/faster way of doing x consistently?" They also will gain ideas from companies in entirely different industries, recognizing the systems and asking themselves: "Should we or can we modify this to benefit our company?"

Why are systems such a big deal? Because, it's easier to replicate systems or processes than it is to replicate people. In fact, it's systems, or the "way things get done" that create the company's future leaders—all built and blessed by the company's current leadership.

Some famous examples of systems-focused businesses are Ray Kroc's McDonald's businesses, Federal Express and Dell Computers. With the exception of McDonald's, these organizations started their business lives as systems-businesses. The result for all of them has been consistent and predictable outcomes-for employees, investors and customers alike.

Focusing on creating systems in your enterprise will generate wealth for both you and the business.

Okay, so what is the first step to creating systems in my business? Start with creating your personal Board of Advisors. I'll go into more detail about boards later on, but in the meanwhile, begin thinking about the many people you know personally, starting with family and friends, and then colleagues. If you look deep enough, you will probably find lawyers, accountants, other business owners, people who specialize or excel at selling, marketing, planning, organizing, etc.

Take a few minutes now and think about the people who are in your life right now that might be able to guide you in selecting the right systems for your business. When I had taken one client of mine through this process, he discovered that there were no fewer than four lawyers, an accountant, a cousin who designed web sites for a living—all within his family of uncles, aunts, cousins and the like!

Unless you are living in a cave, you most likely have people around you right now that can offer you two of the most valuable resources on earth: their time and their knowledge.

Other books on entrepreneuring talk about handling family as investors (money), but I believe the most valuable investment friends and family can make is their willingness to offer their time and knowledge of things they are most strong in. So before you run out and hire a consultant, check your own neighborhood first. You may find that you already have access to valuable expertise right within reach.

It attracts and retains "A" players found throughout the organization

If cash flow is the lifeblood of the enterprise, A-players are its source of oxygen.

For most of the readers, you know an A-player when you see one. The individual tends to be self-motivated, a self-starter, achievement oriented, bright, intelligent, confident and competent in what they are doing. Other employees admire and respect them, customers like them as well. They have dynamic or a calming energy about them, which either excites or soothes others. Companies that have them working for them tend to make a lot of investment in their growth, through training and opportunities to lead.

A-players can't be bought, only invited to play.

The bottom-line is: all great companies have A-players, and they have them because A-players want to be there.

People who place a high value on achievement and growth literally need to work for great companies—or turn the company their working for into one.

Most, if not all entrepreneurs became entrepreneurs as a result of failed attempts to find great companies and great leaders to work for.

It's interesting. I actually started my professional career working for the Smithsonian Institution. The Smithsonian is a great organization, as great as a quasi-government institution can be, and I loved working there, but eventually, the organization simply couldn't provide me enough avenues to grow in—and I eventually left.

One of my mentors, a Director by the name of Claudine Brown, offered me this observation: *"What you're looking for, the Institution is ready or able to provide you, and you are too young so you don't have the political weight to change things in your favor. Although it would be a loss to the Smithsonian, you should give serious consideration to becoming a Management Consultant. It's what you're good at and love to do. Do it."*

Claudine, if you're reading this, thank you for that advice. . .

A-players want to take the winning shot. They're fast studies, and will place smart bets all day long on opportunities that may provide growth to them.

A few years ago while at Envision U the owner and I recently had our quarterly review, which involved assessing and reviewing our systems, strategies and business direction. When we came to the question: *"As a business, how are we really doing?"* The answer was "very well," and it was based on the presence and interest of several A-players that had walked into our doors wanting to be a part of what Envision U was doing.

When you are making the right decisions and you are developing your business to be a great business, A-players will arrive at your doorstep. If you create a business filled with short cuts, a business where it's just about money, you will only attract people that you're going to have problems with in the future.

J. Paul Getty once interviews a promising candidate to head up one of his divisions. The interview goes well, so well in fact, that Getty is ready to hire the candidate on the spot. At some point in the interview, he asks the fellow what were his salary requirements. The candidate replies with a figure that is well below what a person of his experience and capability should be. It's at this point that Getty decides not to hire him, not wanting an executive who under values themselves so...

What's great about attracting and having A-players work for you is that they are natural magnets for other A-players. A-players have friends who are A-players. They have mentors, they have rich personal networks of people and resources, and they utilize these resources every chance they can get.

In talking with my partners, I expressed how excited I was with Envision U's current business phase (Growth, by the way), because of the interest of several A-players. Once a business has attracted one, others are quick to follow. In our case, one particular A-player made their decision to be involved with the company quickly, and even though they've received several unsolicited job offers from several other firms, they have chosen our business to play in, even though it will be some time before we will be ready to bring them on board full-time.

No sooner than a week past, before they began offering the company access to their network of people. The result: We have several A-players to look at and talk to, all referred to us by a single individual.

Why would this person do this? Because they have made an emotional connection with our company. Once they decided that the company was going to be the right vehicle for them to work in—they made it *their company*. A-players treat the company they work in like it was their own. A-players operate like owners (intrapreneurs) of the business. That's why so many become entrepreneurs in the first place—they can't help themselves.

Build a great business, the A-players will find you, and if they really believe in what you are doing, they will go out of their way to find creative ways for the two of you to work together.

You may be asking yourself, what is or what about B-players? At Envision U, because of the business its in (personal development, performance coaching, personal empowerment, performance training), it attracts all kinds of people wanting to play, to be involved in the business in some way. A-players are as I've just described to you—they are the desired resources for any business-period.

B-players are individuals who perform well, but require things outside of themselves to drive their efforts—it could be money, but most likely its constant reassurance, acknowledgement, support and directives provided by management. Your typical 1099-consultant or for-hire professional falls in the B category.

B-level people are competent, valuable (if used correctly), but they don't have an emotional investment—don't really have a care as to whether the business succeeds or fails. B-players are truly employees, expecting direction while A-players want to know how the game is played, and then they just play the game.

C-players we don't even want to fool with; they are interested, not committed, they are expensive and don't deliver enough value against what will ultimately be invested-your hard earned cash...

An easy way to recognize A-players when they walk in the door:

- You immediately sense their positive energy
- When discussing what they have done or are doing career-wise, they talk a lot from a relationship or team basis: "Together, we achieved...The company has succeeded in..."
- They ask probing and intelligent questions about your business, its needs. More importantly, they listen intently to your responses.
- Use the word "We," vs. "I"—a lot

The most telling sign that you are in the presence of an A-player is the discussion you have with them, where all you here is what "we can do..." statements. "I" statements are rarely heard, unless you are probing them for something specific, whereas B-players; all they talk about is what they did, what "I accomplished." Both display confidence, but the person that acknowledges that most things done in business involve others—is the stronger, more desirable find.

B-players are experts, at least that's the identity they want to have. They spend their time assuring you that they do indeed know what they are doing. They say all the right things, but more than likely you will need people around you who are emotionally connected with what they're doing in the business—B-players won't go there, in fact, they are quick to leave a situation that requires this.

Most consultants, and other freelance professionals play in this space. For them, they trade expertise for money-nothing more, but sometimes less.

Companies like Envision U, are always prepared to use consultants, in fact I started off as a high-level consultant to the company, but we were very careful in who we selected to engage with. As a rule, we delegated the most technical-oriented and monotonous tasks we could find to consultants, and tried to only engage consultants who were willing to work on a fixed fee, project-based structure, and we financially penalized consultants who missed project timelines, through no delay on our own.

It seems harsh, but if you study this further, you will see the wisdom in this. Only the best of the best would take on an engagement with these conditions. Did we pay a lot for this? Often, we paid fair market value for services provided and sometimes a slight premium if the projects rapid. What we found was that the best consultants appreciated the no-nonsense, no-haggle, direct approach we had to contracting services. The engagements typically went off smoothly and deliverables were met, because we negotiated in advance the timeline with the consultant, and the best of them never lie dabout what they could do and when.

If you find yourself having to work with consultants, especially in the beginning of launching your enterprise, find consultants that are competent enough in their craft that they will accept a fixed-fee vs. hourly arrangement. Some of you may feel this locks you in somehow, and that hourly is better. No, it's not: With the former, you pay *upon completion of project*, with the latter; *you pay as the project unfolds*. We've heard countless horror stories of small business owners paying hundreds, sometimes *thousands* of dollars in consulting fees, only to not have a finished product.

When does an hourly arrangement make sense? When the project is a relatively small, or the work is not involved enough (and thus not lucrative enough) to interest elite consultants—and you still want to outsource the work. Expect to pay a higher hourly rate for a consultant, a good not desperate consultant to take it on.

Remember J. Paul Getty's experience: You get what you pay for, and a person's sense of self-worth must *match or exceed* what you would expect to pay.

It has a very profitable and deep customer base

We all understand that, without customers, there is no business. This is a universal truth, but another truth is that to have a great business one must have great customers. Customers willing to continually make investments (purchases) in your company's products and services over and over again, at a level where profit is realized.

There are two schools of thought: The first, believes that companies should be perpetually marketing-- constantly replenishing the customers that drop off the radar. The theory behind this being that customer bases naturally decay or decline over time. The second believes that a company's main focus and major investments should be in its existing customers, the customers that have proven themselves (read: purchase frequently) with the company over time.

Should you do one and not the other? Well, no, but you will need to determine where the bulk of your sales dollars are going to go. Should you use your cash to chase and court a prospective customer, or should you devise a way to invest in your existing customers where additional profit is realized?

The answer is: it depends. It depends on the type of customers you have and the type of business you are in. In the chapter on "Managing the Enterprise," I will go into greater detail about customers, but if you have Tier I customers, it is generally wise that you divert the bulk of your sales dollars to cultivating this existing customer base.

In brief, Tier I customers are your company's most profitable customers. Their needs, desires, and challenges fit perfectly with your company's product or service offering. They are completely sold on what your company is about, and freely purchase the next product or service you have to offer, and they're often grateful for what your business has done for them, and in fact, when key people move on to work for other companies, you'll often get a call from them, wanting to do this all over again. When looking at your numbers, you find that a large percentage of your revenues come from this group.

The average small business may have just one Tier I customer. In many cases, it is the first one; that early customer that took a liking to you, or who mentored your start. And the average small business typically overtime fails to sustain and build on this, having spent all of their energy time and money chasing real customers, vs. learning to cultivate the good ones they already have.

When I was working at the Smithsonian, just across the street in front of the Castle, was a hotdog vendor named Marie. For as long as I can remember working at the Smithsonian, Marie has been there faithfully in her little spot on the sidewalk. Anyway, myself and many other government types regularly purchased lunch and other items from her, but what Marie really provided was a sense of familiarity and connection.

With her Tier I customers, she took the time to learn your name, knew your kids name, what kind of work you did, when you last had a vacation... So with your purchase, she gave you the added value of being recognized, and ultimately appreciated enough that she acknowledged you by name. In fact, the connection she provided often resulted in people just stopping by to say hello, even if they weren't buying anything that day or moment. In any case, she was consistent and you were always acknowledged and thus respected.

Well, one day the inevitable happened—a competing stand showed up and set up just 12 feet away. This vendor had all the bells and whistles—almost twice the variety of offering and in some cases—lower prices. Tier I customers to the rescue....While Marie lost nearly all of her Tier II customers (tourist mainly), just about all of her top customers stood fast and loyal. It was amazing. I remember being out on a nice afternoon day, eating outside, and seeing for a solid hour *lines* of regulars at Marie's little booth, buying all kinds of things, well beyond "the usual." Marie, pleasant as always, seemed unfazed by the other vendor's presence. She didn't change a thing—didn't dicker around with pricing, no fancy additional products. She just continued to acknowledge her customers and provide the service we all came to expect. After three weeks of this, the other vendor was no where to be found...

The best companies have great customers.
Establish your business so that it attracts these customers.

It has the right resources deployed in the right way at the right time

The right resources at the right time... For small business owners, the correct use of cash flow can be a tricky thing. Entrepreneurs are constantly weighing the pros and cons of purchasing equipment, hiring people, running the ad, going to this convention or that. For some it's part of the rush, for others it can be a daunting task that never seems to get easier. Again: your personal board to the rescue.

Unfortunately, there is no magic formula. Each business has it's own particular "season" or cycle. If for example you are in the lawn care business or say gift basket business, then your business is seasonal, where you make most of your money in just a portion of the calendar year. Several entrepreneurs I've spoken with on this matter believe that cash preservation is a top priority. "Be quick to save and slow to spend," they say in a nutshell. Again, if you look at everything you do as an investment, you should be okay. For every dollar you spend, you expect a dollar or more in return.

One of the most important things you can do is to track where the cash goes. If you can afford a bookkeeper, even if just part-time, that can go a long way towards helping you control the flow of cash. For those of you willing to take it on yourself, Intuit's QuickBooks™ and Quicken for Personal & Business Finance™ software are great basic tools for doing this. Whatever system you choose, just make sure you choose something, especially early on to help you manage the cash.

We can't leave this section without talking about the trickiest of all resources to time: *hiring people.*

So you've launched your business, things are going great, and you come to realize that you need to start hiring a few people. The common mistake many entrepreneurs just starting out make is that they hire their friends, and hire people they like, over hiring people that can fulfill a need. Be careful when hiring friends and especially family. It's natural that you would want those closest to you in your business, but that friend or family member may not be the most ideally suited to the current *need* of your business. Sometimes, the best person for the job isn't someone you'd necessarily hang out with after work, but they have the skills and qualities to get the job done. Working with friends and family can be a precarious affair, especially when you have to manage, critique and possibly reprimand their performance. Try to avoid the trap of just hiring people like yourself and instead hire what you need.

It is designed to be very cash flow efficient

For every business owner, cash is a very big deal. If cash is a big deal, then it's management is an even bigger deal. The lack of management of cash flow is where a lot of promising and potentially successful companies get into trouble—trouble that many never recover from. Some of the more common scenarios involve: taking on too much payroll, miss timing the use of credit lines (bank credit lines, credit cards, personal loans), and buying too much capital equipment (computers, office furniture, that neat postage machine, the $400 executive's chair, etc.) too soon, but the number one cash killer is underestimating the cost of servicing won business.

Those of you playing in the government-contracting arena can probably attest to this. I can almost see your heads nodding in agreement. It seems odd I'm sure, but really winning business is a fairly easy thing to do, when compared to fulfilling your obligation to the business that's won. If you are selling a product, it may be a little easier to anticipate and know what the costs are, but if you have a service business, it can be a bit more complicated.

How do you make a business more cash flow efficient? Well, the first thing to realize is that it is an ongoing concern—the best companies work constantly at being efficient with its resources—especially cash. Companies in a proactive mode expend great effort to be more efficient with cash before they need to do so.

Companies that take a reactive approach, find that they have to lay people off, that they can't get an extension on existing credit lines or can't secure new lines of credit, and find their profit, *both realized, and unrealized*—in jeopardy. Companies in a reactive mode, wait until it's necessary before they take action on managing cash flow.

My advice is: **don't wait.** Be aggressive with how you manage cash now, when cash is flowing easily. Invest early in systems; establish great procedures (rules) early as to how your company deals with profit, with credit, payroll, taxes and purchases. The easiest time to do so is always before you need to. Take full advantage of this, and do it now. For this to work, everyone in the enterprise must operate on the same level, in terms of how the company values, respects and manages cash.

It is a business, which can grow and be grown for the right reasons

Do you remember the beanie babies and pokemon craze of just a few years ago? These were business concepts that profited by exploiting fads and the latest curiosities of our time. But then there are businesses whose value, product and service stand the test of time. Where does your business fit?

In general, you want to consider businesses that have ample growth potential, and thus enough time for stakeholders to realize a return (profit). Businesses which exploit a fad are okay too, but it can be a tricky undertaking: there is a great risk of staying in the game too long, making one too many reinvestments in inventory/product creation. Betting on a fad business is like betting on a race horse running a quarter-mile track: the horse is good for maybe one or two races, and then should be retired.

MLMs or multi-level-marketing business concepts are similar in nature to fad businesses. Why? Because MLMs have a distinctive cycle: those who are early participants in a new MLM, stand to make the most money when the MLM peaks, in terms of the number of people involved. Eventually, all MLMs reach a saturation point, and anyone who comes on board at that time is faced with a decaying market.

Fad businesses operate the same: there is only one Beanie baby company, there is only one Pokemon company, and while there are now many copycats, the bulk of the run and profit were realized by these two companies and there stakeholders (collectors). Building a

-78-

business with a limited life expectancy is okay: just realize that's what it is: a short-run play for profit. Building a business that has near unlimited growth potential allows for the highest probability of profit for its stakeholders. The choice is yours...

It provides distinct value for its customers, at an advantage over other competitors

Great companies provide exceptional value to its customers. This value can be reflected in many ways. Perhaps you have tailored your product or service to address a specific need of one of your Tier I customers. Possibly your company has made a considerable investment in really understanding this customer's business, to the point that your product or service helps them create value to *their customers*. Maybe your company and its customers have created such a strong relationship or establish such great rapport that together you've developed a unique service or product that both companies profit from.

The possibilities for how distinct value is created are unlimited. Clearly, both the costs (risks) and the reward (profit) are potentially high, but because you are making this investment with your Tier I customer, it's worth the risk; it's worth the investment.

Every superior company seeks to turn their best customers into partners. Creating value like this is the way this can occur-- all at the advantage over other competitors. Why can't they compete against this? Because this level of value creation is based upon the relationship between company and customer and it can't be attacked with price. Remember the hot dog vendor, Marie? She created intrinsic value above and beyond her product, and as a result, the competing vendor failed in capturing her market—because it's not just about price. In fact, with the best companies and customers—it's never about price; it's about value.

It is a business focused on creating value through innovation

Regardless of the business you're in, ultimately, innovation plays a part in its ongoing success. Innovation in terms of the type of processes you use to deliver your product or service; the way it hires people, manages customers. The best companies focus on growing profit in two directions: thru increases in revenues and decreasing expenses.

Innovation and efficiency go hand in hand, and it is an objective that most superior enterprises strive for. If you are just starting out, establish the practice of innovation early in your business. Learn to be efficient before you have to.

It competes in the marketplace as a proactive business vs. reactive business

The most important and valuable thing I can advise you to consider is to be certain yours is a proactive business. Proactive businesses are constantly pushing the envelope. These businesses actively evaluate previously effective strategies, methods, policies and procedures, to see if they are still valid. Leaders running these businesses are perfectly willing to "rock the boat," to make a perfectly good business even better.

These businesses change and adapt *before they have to*. Companies built and operated around innovation tend to be very proactive in their approach and attitude towards change. And for many, it can be a very effective counter-measure against competition.

A great example of this is Asigra, Inc., a great company based out of Canada. I had the privilege of meeting with its founder recently. Asigra offers state-of-the-art data storage and recovery software, which competes head-on with the giants in the industry. What's interesting about Asigra's business is that it's technology, considered cutting edge today and was created over six years ago. Okay, so they were ahead of their time, but what's really amazing is that the advance features, considered innovations today were also conceived and developed many years ago.

Understanding the customer, Asigra's founder was wise enough to offer just the basic foundation of the technology, and over time, as the market became comfortable and efficient with it, he slowly introduced these "advanced features" into the foundation product, thus guaranteeing that the Asigra solution is seen as a leading innovator in its industry.

Another reason for this strategy was to help Asigra manage its would-be competitors. Competitors who are bigger with more resources, which could quickly and easily replicate Asigra's offering. When the founder talked of this, he had a large smile on his face. "When my competitor does this, they inadvertently signal to the marketplace that the Asigra solution is valid and the way to go."

Asigra stops its competitors right in their tracks, because they are always copying old news. Asigra manages their impact, by timely release of advance features. The result is that many would-be competitors have resigned to license Asigra's technology, vs. copy or attack it.

It is a business, which rewards all stakeholders

As my good friend Nancy Curtis puts it: "Business is about people and providing value to them." A business has many masters, stakeholders.

The obvious stakeholders are its owners, investors, employees, but there are also, creditors, customers, vendors, business-to-business partners, the media, the community that the business operates in, the families of everyone directly or indirectly supported or involved. Essentially, every human being who is directly or indirectly impacted by the business's existence is a stakeholder.

This book is meant for those leaders operating businesses with their stakeholders in mind. The very best try to make business decisions that create value for all. Again, I look to Warren Buffet, who has over 50 managers, all very wealthy and who don't need to work another day for the rest of their lives, whose singular focus is to protect the interest of it's stakeholders and create value for all to benefit from. You might be thinking that it's far easier to just focus on yourself, your own interest, and in many instances you would be correct—it would be. But as Nancy indicated early, it's about people.

There are times when it seems impossible, this business you're in. Everything is hard, the right decision isn't clear, but a decision must be made, a path chosen. The only way to know for certain if your business is really sound occurs when it's tested. Tested with a crisis or turning point. During these times, your people, the support of everyone involved in the enterprise becomes extremely important, extremely valuable. And if you have led your organization with your people in mind-they will rally behind you and together, you will accomplish what no one individual could; you will survive the crisis and thrive as a result of it.

Be the leader who places the needs, desires and concerns of its stakeholders above the one. You will be amply rewarded.

For those of you currently running a company, take a moment and compare your business against these attributes. In what areas is your business weak? What resources do you need to acquire? Is your business the kind that great people are attracted to work for? Are you pursuing the right customer? Does your company spend its time and energy reacting to your competitors? Are you cash efficient?

CHAPTER IV

The Business Architect:

Designing the Enterprise

Business architecture is like composing a symphony. It begins with a grand concept or a great idea, and it's the business architect's job to interpret this concept and translate it into a common business language. The language of words, numbers, diagrams, pictures, analogies, stories: this is what it takes to provide a score or blueprint from which everyone else can build upon.

The inception phase of any business is the domain of the business architect. A rare breed of entrepreneur, people exhibiting this trait tend to be highly structured, organized in their thinking, actions, behaviors and in the way they process things. The best of the group tend to be highly creative and imaginative in both idea generation and problem solving.

At the inception phase of any endeavor, you're establishing the groundwork: setting the vision and mission of this new concept; creating the plans and objectives. You are also beginning to identify what resources are available and what resources are still needed.

As you begin the process of exploring the concept, assembling the pieces, doing the research, gathering information, you see the concept starting to take form. If you have an Architect involved, you can take that added step and design the concept, starting at the end, meaning starting with what you will ultimately have, and work your way back to the beginning.

Some of the key factors involved during the Inception phase of the business are:

- Have the right reasons for creating the enterprise
- Plan with the "Exit" in mind
- Know the risk(s) involved
- Determine the outcomes (revenues, impact, size, etc.)
- Identify the strengths and weaknesses of the business concept
- Designing a risk management plan (establishing the business rules)
- Estimating the cost to pursue it (the business)
- Commitment

Let's look briefly at each one...

Have the right reasons for creating the enterprise

It is really important that you are creating the enterprise for the right reasons. Some of the *right reasons* are:

- You have identified a want, need or desire that is currently being unfulfilled, and you have a product or service that's meets this.
- You have identified a business that you strongly believe you can succeed in, because of your existing professional or personal experience or expertise.

- You've been offered an opportunity, in which you believe that you can create a sustainable and profitable business around

Some of the *wrong reasons* would be:
- Doing it to prove to someone that you can run a business
- Doing it because you've always fantasized about being your own boss.
- Doing it because you believe you can get rich quick
- Getting into business because of ego, or to compete with say a relative or friend.

What should drive your decision to even pursue building a business: your passion, your level of interest and commitment, your knowledge and your belief that there is a market for your product or service, and that you can deliver it at a profit.

Plan with the 'Exit' in mind

Sometimes, it can be very helpful during your planning to begin with the end result or exit in mind. Your "exit" could be that you take the company public, that you sell the business privately, or that you install a team to run it while you go off and travel the world. There are an infinite number of exit scenarios, and the exit can change, depending on how the business develops, but for planning purposes, pick one, and build with it in mind.

Operating your business with the exit in mind, serves as a beacon to help guide and direct your decisions. Knowing your exit helps support your guidance mechanism, to steer the venture in the right direction and help you stay the course.

Know the risk(s) involved

Risk and being an entrepreneur are synonymous. Sometimes, it is very difficult to determine what the risks are in a business concept, but you would do well to try and determine what they are *in advance of your launch.*

Risk can be found at any level within the business model. Such risk factors include cash flow, demand, cost to produce your product or cost to deliver your service, tax considerations, people, the location of your business, business identity, startup cost, litigation risk, over-reliance on other vendors or suppliers, and the list goes on and on. The best time to cast a clear eye on any potential risk is now, before the doors are open and the money clock has started.

Determine the outcomes (revenues, impact, size, etc.)

Determining the outcomes for the business. How big do you envision the business eventually being? Are you still running the company, if say, you decide to take it public? What type of revenue levels are you expecting in one year? In three years? In five years? What is the impact of your business in the market space? How many employees?

Again, this is one of the best times to really consider these things, before the pressure of operating a running business sets in. You want to determine your outcomes and set your vision for the company, because you can't hit the bull's-eye on a target that you haven't even defined.

Identify the strengths and weaknesses of the business concept

Be honest. Be brutal. Think carefully: What are the strengths or pluses to my business concept? How strong of a concept is it? Are there already customers clamoring for this product or service? Are there many competitors, or only a few? If there are only a few, am I missing something—possibly some barrier to entry that I don't know about? Is the concept something that results in having loyal, repeat customers?

And don't forget the weaknesses: Is the concept a flash in the pan, a fad product or service? Is there enough profit to justify even offering it? Does the concept allow me to create a business that's distinctly unique when compared to others?

A quick example: If you compare say, owning a car dealership or having a dentist practice specializing in invisible braces, which do you believe would be more profitable? It depends, right? Okay how about this: Which would you say would generate the most profit on a per-customer basis, from among their *repeat customers*?

The answer is: the dealership, because, cars wear out—eventually, a car owner will replace, trade in, sell or junk their old car and purchase a new one, and if the dealership did their job by establishing good rapport, they should end up getting or at least having the opportunity to sell them another car. Whereas, for the dentist specialist, once a patient has purchased whatever system to get their teeth straight—they're done. For the dealership, there will always be that mix of new and repeat customers. For the dental specialist, the majority of their customers will have to be new customers.

Designing a risk management plan (establishing the business rules)

One of the keys to keeping the business vehicle together, to surviving the opportunities, the challenges, the unexpected sale or loss, is to establish the business rules, the rules of play.

Some of the questions you might find yourself considering are: How do we handle excess cash? What is our approach to handling credit lines? What is a good customer? What kind of sales situation is one we should walk away from? What steps would we need to take if we suddenly lost 50% of our average monthly revenues? What if we doubled our average monthly revenues? What situation or set of circumstances would justify getting an office? Moving to a new office?

Realize that the rules will change as the business or its environment and opportunities change. As leaders of your enterprise, you will be constantly considering new rules and validating old ones. Begin the process now at the planning stage.

Estimating the cost to pursue it

Essentially, what is it going to take to launch the business? Money, manpower, time, energy?. What would it take to operate with $0 profit for two years? What are the upfront costs? What are the reoccurring costs?

The work you do with your business plan, whether it's a formal encyclopedia length tomb, or a streamlined 10-page document; your findings will help you determine what the costs are.

Commitment

When the excitement has passed, and it's work now, do you believe that you have what it takes to stick to it? To stay the course, even when the business is rocked by a bit of good fortune, or bad?

You must have a certain level of commitment to see things through. Often, the reward in a business is farther away than planned for or expected. In many cases, the greater the reward, the more complex the enterprise, and thus the longer it takes for the return to be realized. Oil drill riggers from the past come to mind here. They've done the surveying, and their gut says there is oil to be found here, so much so, they commit to drilling the dig, only to quit three feet from the "gold."

Launching a business is very much like drilling for oil or digging for gold; sometimes, after all the preliminary work has been done, you just have to dig. Dig knowing there's oil or gold, even though you can't see it yet.

That's really the key difference between mediocre entrepreneurs and great ones. The great ones commit to their vision and stick to the course—they dig, *even without proof.*

I'll see it *when I believe it,* is their mantra...

Well, at this point, let's take a break from the concepts and get into a few real world situations.

Let me take you into the world of a fellow colleague and Architect entrepreneur, Akhil Thapliyal.

Akhil was born in India in 1964, but being a son of a prominent ambassador, he considers himself a child of the world. I met Akhil several years ago, while working as a consultant. Being true to form, he was the chief engineer there, and without his assistance and interest, my project would have failed massively. I was very fortunate to get his support early.

When I asked him later what made him decide to support me and the project I was running he replied, "I could tell immediately that you knew your stuff, and when I asked you a few technical questions on some things you didn't know about, you were honest with me. Right then and there, I decided to help you."

Well, I survived that project, a project that was designed to fail for political reasons, but succeed we did. Akhil and I have been good friends ever since. Shortly after that escapade, he shared with me his concept for Labyrinth Technologies. At the time, it was a very ambitious undertaking, and the concept intrigued me, so I elected to assist him with the planning. Typical of most concepts, the inevitable delays occurred, such that it wasn't until this year that Akhil could position the concept to launch it. In the three-year delay, he has continued to fine-tune and modify the business premise to match current business conditions. In addition, he has been selectively and methodically building his core team of people to deliver the Labyrinth solution.

What's extraordinary about Akhil is that while he is essentially an architect at heart, he is also very adept at team building, a rare trait among architects. His power comes from his ability to focus on the team, and he's very efficient in his strategies and planning, particularly when seeking a solution to a problem.

Being a typical Architect, he has a voracious appetite for knowledge and growth. There have been many evenings where he and I have been in deep discussions on a wide range of topics from human psychology to the concept of joy.

Akhil. Tell us a little bit about Labyrinth Technologies.

Labyrinth Technologies is a services company, which offers its customers business applications and custom developed solutions for their enterprise-all delivered from an Internet browser. We provide a complete solution for those businesses that truly want to be internet-based, from data storage to shared applications and work collaboration.

Our service offering is designed using state-of-the-art technology to deliver this, and deliver it securely. In addition to this, Labyrinth also offers traditional, high-level, enterprise level engineering and re-engineering services. With our engineering services, we help navigate our clients to achieving true return on investments on their existing technology. As you know from your own experience in the field, there are a lot of poorly designed networks out there.

Yes. I made a small fortune, coming into these clients to correct a lot of poor designs. In terms of your business concept, I remember discussing this with you years ago, what has taken so long? And how have you been able to patiently wait for the right opportunity to launch the business?

Well, if you recall, a major portion of Labyrinth's internet-delivery architecture had to be designed, tested. And we were reliant on some of Novell's advanced technology. With new products, there are always unexpected delays. In many ways, the technology we needed for our design simply wasn't mature enough; wasn't ready. I had a decision to make: either I wait for Novell to build the feature sets Labyrinth required, or I could spend Labyrinth's capital and develop it ourselves.
I remember discussing this with you. What did you decide?

Ultimately, I decided to stay the course and not divert capital allocated for building Labyrinth's team and instead, worked with Novell and their senior developers directly to gauge their progress. Fortunately, the technology turned out to be sound-we were just a bit too early to incorporate it into our business model, but now it's ready.

Did you receive any unexpected benefit from the delay? And how important was having a sound plan and strategy set for Labyrinth to you?

We benefited like none other. In the three to four years, Labyrinth has been very active with development and marketing activities with Novell, such that Labyrinth is well positioned to be a flagship business showcasing advanced usage of some of Novell's core web-technologies.

We didn't have this three years ago. Also, I've had time to really refine some of the core strategies in terms of Labyrinth's offering. I've also been fortunate to discover several really amazing people to include in the core team. And finally, I know more, and have a better idea as to the kind of value I want Labyrinth to create for it's clientele.

As for the importance of planning and strategy-it is extremely important, especially given the kind of delays we've experienced. In three years, I saw the dot-com industry blow up, experienced the economic impact of 9/11, Enron, economic slow-down. All very profound experiences that impacted my thinking and approach to this business.

In my case, having a pre-determined plan and strategy has kept the business concept alive in my mind, and has allowed me to work around the wait, while still making small progress towards launching.

That's fantastic. With Labyrinth Technologies, you are operating as it's chief designer and builder. Can you tell our readers how important teams are to your business?

What's the point in winning if there is no one else around to enjoy the spoils with you? I've always wanted to create a business and have my friends around me. You know, we work hard, and we play hard. It's easy working by yourself, but that's not as interesting to me as in making a team work, and work well. Essentially, I'm a fire fighter: it's what I do best.

What you most enjoy doing...

Yes, what I enjoy doing. I probably will always be a fire fighter to some extent. All for one- one for all. Everyone has a role to play, everyone is equally important. We are all playing with the same end goal in mind—to win. Teams are a very big deal.

Four years ago, I thought the first team I would be building for Labyrinth would be its core team that I have always envisioned. But do to circumstances I had to focus instead on building Labyrinth's external team first. By external team I mean working with the Novell's, IBM's and Cisco's of the world. Focusing on them first turned out to be very fortunate for me.

I suppose in many ways they are early investors in Labyrinth?

Absolutely. What's cool is that, with a few modifications, our business model became very compelling to these vendors-- Especially with so many tech business failures that have occurred. I can now reach the Regional VP of Marketing for Novell, and propose very creative co-marketing ideas with her—and she's listening. Three years ago, that would not have been possible.

One door closes, another opens…

Yes.

Speaking of doors, what is your exit strategy for Labyrinth?

Well, you know I would like Labyrinth Technologies to last forever, but I see Labyrinth staying privately held. I'm considering positioning the company to sell it to the employees. I think the business is too complex and profitable to take public, and I have no interest in running a publicly traded company. It's also possible that I may sell it to one of our strategic partners. Ultimately, it would have to be sold to a buyer that understood the technology of the business.

How are you handling the capitalization of your business?

Well, business development has largely been self-funded. Novell, IBM and others have been very supportive, providing Labyrinth with access to key technologies, developers and other resources. About 80% of Labyrinth's technology has been deployed within several of my personal clients

If there is anything that I could impart on your readers it's this: really focus on establishing great relationships by creating value, especially for those who demonstrate early on, that they believe in you and in what you are doing.

Thanks Akhil.

You're very welcome.

In Summary:

For those of you running or considering creating businesses, please consider the power and benefit that planning might offer you. In the case of my friend, Akhil, without planning it is quite possible that his company launch would never had occurred.

Because he invested the time and energy early in creating a formal plan for his business, he was able to fine-tune it to benefit from the many changes and opportunities that presented it, and he was able to create value towards his business, even though he was faced with nearly a four-year delay in launching the business.

Does this mean that you have to go out and create a 70-page business plan? Not necessarily. At a minimum, you should be able to answer the following questions.

What purpose does my business serve? (What business are we in?)

Who benefits from my business? (Customers, partners, community, family, etc.)

What resources (knowledge, tools, people, etc) are needed to do the business?

What is the cost for launching the business? (time, money, effort)
What is the risk in creating the business? (time, money, effort)

Who do I know that can assist me? (Board of Advisors, mentors, friends)

Is my business unique, and if so does this uniqueness give my business an edge over the competition?

Why do I want to do this business?

Am I prepared to do what it takes to see it through?

Do I have a passion for this business? Does it compliment what I already do well?

One of the main values to preparing a business plan is that it forces you to really address the tough questions. Create a plan or don't, your choice of course—just be sure you ask the tough questions. Ask them early, ask often, but be certain to ask.

CHAPTER V

The Business Builder:
Creating the Enterprise

"The Master is available to all people and doesn't reject anyone. He is ready to use all situations and doesn't waste anything..." –Lao-tzu

When thinking of the building phase of the enterprise, a movie phrase comes to mind: "It was the best of times, and the worst of times…" For most people, when they fantasize about what it would be like to run their own business, this is the phase they think about. With planning out of the way (if that even occurred), now we get to the stuff that gets most people's juices flowing. As I've mentioned earlier, this is the most exciting time, because it's still new and there is plenty of action, plenty of things to look at and be excited by.

You've got your business cards in hand, maybe you even have an office or you've placed that first advertisement. This is it! You're in business!" You envision all of the customers who will clamor for your product or service, you visualize all of the money you will see coming your way. This is the stuff that great dreams are made from, and it is the realm of the Builder.

The building phase of an enterprise represents the enterprises' and it's leaders' initiation into being. In this phase, you are publicly announcing your existence. It is here that you begin to learn what your business and you as a leader are made out of. With your first customer, your testing begins. You will begin to see things which answer questions that you may be asking yourself like: "Is this thing going to work?" "Are there customers for this, and will they buy from us?" "Will I make money?" And, "Will we make it?" For many, it's exciting and it feels like you are traveling in a whirlwind. Things happen either very quickly or at a snail's pace.

But regardless, the enterprise begins its life here and like an Olympic baton race, having a good start is paramount to finishing well.

At this point, I'll introduce someone who knows a good deal about building and operating within whirlwinds. In this past year, I've had the privilege of becoming close friends with an exceptional human being and savvy businesswoman. Her name is Nancy Curtis, and she is CEO of Credo Technologies, Inc.

Her story is an interesting one: Like many of us, she started out as an intrapreneur, working in the Intelligence community, intrapreneuring her way quickly through the ranks. In her last sortie as an employee/intrapreneur, she identified a need with information management that currently was unfulfilled.

Confident that she could design a solution, she made the leap, deciding to leave a 20-year career and venture out on her own. What's truly interesting is that she is blazing a new trail in what until now has been un-chartered territory. When I asked if she would be willing to share her story, she gladly accepted. Take good notes, ladies and gentlemen, there is a million dollars worth of wisdom heading your way.

Nancy, thanks for taking the time to talk with my readers. This is very valuable.

No problem, Chris. I'm happy to share whatever I can, you know that.

Yes, and I really appreciate it. Okay, so tell us: what is *InfoSeer* all about?

InfoSeer builds state-of-the-art software products that is the "informational sentinel" to controlling, protecting and watching information wherever it goes. We provide the raw material to any industry that treats information as a valuable asset, one worth protecting.

As I've gotten to know you this past year, it was interesting to learn how InfoSeer came to exist. Take us through this, beginning from your days as an Intrapreneur.

Well, I basically began intrapreneuring within, working for a large company. And all throughout my career, I've been very successful in building something from nothing. Building business when there wasn't any business to be had. I've always sort of built my own success ladder, and basically have always worked for large enterprises. The last just prior to InfoSeer, I was hired to create a business unit for an integrator that wanted to break into the intelligence community. I was successful in doing so, and through this effort, I discovered a void, which I thought could be addressed if someone took the time to do so. And InfoSeer was born.

That's fantastic. Did you have any mentors along the way? Were you impacted by mentors?

I did have some significant ones. When I first started out of college, I had a very significant mentor at BDM, who sort of took me under his wing.

In this case, this mentor was looking for a certain type of individual to design and implement new systems and improve upon others, to take the enterprise to a new level of growth and performance. Based upon your book, he was definitely the Architect type intrapreneur, and he needed a catalyst to get it all done.

But you were right out of college, correct?

Yes. I think in this case it was a plus, because I would only be bringing new ideas and energy to this, and he didn't have to worry about undoing anything I might have picked up from other companies.

Still, he was taking a risk.

Yes, but it was calculated. Really the things I eventually implemented only a person with no limitations could have created. His risk was that I wouldn't deliver, but that's a risk you take with each new hire.

Well, obviously you delivered. Were you both successful? Was the objective met?

I think so. A lot of innovation occurred, the teams responded and were able to perform at a higher level, and he did ultimately transform the business, so I think the objectives were met. Like myself, he has since moved on.

As all intrapreneurs eventually do. What was the main gift he gave you as an advisor?

He basically pulled me right to the top-from day one. He introduced me to a lot of the senior people in the business and really pushed me into understanding how executives work, how they think, and basically set the framework for me that I was never junior.

That was a key thing for me: I never had to deal with the experience of being junior level, and I was pulled right into the next job at a very high level. I was at the same level, already at a senior position.

Outstanding. Back to the present: does your family have any role to play, in terms of your career?

They are very supportive; they like the fact that I have a career; they're happy about that, but as far as interacting with me day to day on the business, no. My husband is very supportive of me, and being involved in real estate, certainly understands the risks and complexity of running a business. He is my sounding board, my council, but no one is actively involved in the business.

What specifically led you to create InfoSeer?

Well, two things. One, was this ability to really be able to create business. To have a vision and to know how to differentiate ourselves from the market space. So why was I able to build something externally? Because I knew the strengths and weaknesses of the competition; I knew what the customer needed; I knew how to differentiate ourselves from the market space and I was very good at it. And so, in the market space I was working in, the intelligence community, they basically rely on methodologies to protect information.

But there was this 'big hole' in sort of this protection as information was moving, when people are looking at it, and I felt that that was a true market, that if the intelligence community was having this problem, then certainly the rest of the world, corporate America was as well.

That's what I see happening now. So it stems from a passion and belief that this was a true need, and understanding the market, working in a closed intelligence community, I could look around the big companies that I was working with and see that they also had no control of their sensitive information, and it really drove me to see that this is something that's really needed in the market space.

Excellent. Was there anyone from that community that supported you in this?

Yes. Some of the people that joined InfoSeer's board were from large companies that operated in the intelligences community. Also, along the way, we had senior people from the intelligence community that came in and supported us and really helped us evolve our product.

It's interesting that you've mentioned your board. In the book, we talk about the importance of having boards. What led you to create your board? How did you know this was the thing to do?

A couple of things really. One, it's one thing to understand the technology and what you are trying to do and have a vision for this. But if you really think about it, if you do a market assessment, and you think about where does our product play in each of these markets—I mean, we did not have expertise in the markets that we knew we needed to play in. Every company can't know everything, so we looked to our board to really bring that expertise to us.

We looked to our board not only for this expertise, but also to help us with market understanding; understanding what's important in that market and help us gain access to some of the key people in that market.

Boards can be very powerful when utilized this way. Interesting. What does InfoSeer offer its board members in return for all of this?

In our case, I gave them stock, so they basically received stock options into the company. I know a lot of people don't do that, and I know it's basically no longer seen in a desirable fashion, due to the dot com wave and bust and the tons of worthless paper as a result. So today, I know that it probably wouldn't be necessary to offer stock, but the reason I've done this is that I wanted them to want to participate; not just participate as an advisor, but I wanted them to say: "If this company is successful, and I give good advice to them because of my success, I want them to benefit from this," so it's sort of a win-win for everybody. And so I would do it again: I would definitely offer stock options today.

Out of the following areas: Market focus, Strategy focus, People focus, and Results (profit), which do you invest most of your time in?

Well, it all kind of comes together. You have to focus on results: So when you start a company at this phase, when you are building a company, you have to think about what results do you want to get? Both in terms of what product or service you're trying to build and offer and how you bring that together. So the results you are seeking are really key, because they sort of drive what you build your strategy around. So if I want to get to point X or I want to build this kind of capability, this is the strategy I have to have to do that.

And the people of course are very important. One of the things that entrepreneurs have to understand when you start a company is: It's not just about the team within your company, it's about the people all around you: people that are working with you, people that are outside like your customers, potential customers, and its your inside team, such as your advisors.

So, when we think about what's the most important, it is that you have to have goals and results that you're targeting for and then you have to spend time getting your team focusing on how we are going to get there and what's the best way to get there? So it's a combination that comes together, but for me it's laying out the results that we're wanting, and then creating the visions, strategies and thinking about the people and resources I'll need to achieve them.

Hum. Regarding people, how have you been able to attract such great people? Is there anything special that you do to attract them to the company?

I have to say some of it is luck (laughter). You know, you get linked up along the way with someone who's phenomenal, and then they refer other phenomenal people to you, and it grows that way. It's really a combination of things that led us to having great people. Being at the right place, because it wasn't by advertising. Everyone who came to us and has worked with us has been through a relationship of knowing somebody.

So it's mainly through your personal network of relationships, but part of that's just lucky, finding amazing people and great people to work with. Maybe as a company, we are open to that, since we are looking for those kinds of people, looking for a certain type of energy and interest. But we do not do the blind Internet job board search. For us, our group came about through who people knew.

That's a great explanation and strategy. I know my readers will appreciate your acknowledging luck being somewhat of a factor. But I also think great businesses ultimately attract great people.

Yes, I think that's true.

Yes. Okay, knowing you both personally and professionally, I know that you have both a business and a personal life. How have you manage to have both?

Well you know, when you start your own company, they kind of melt together, so it's very important for the spouse to be supportive. Because, if I came home and my husband was not interested at all in listening to my business, hearing what my day was about, or letting me debrief my strategies and I had to keep them in those 16-hour day periods it would be very difficult. But the fact is that we both enjoy hearing about each other's day and talking about our businesses, which helps to meld our personal and professional lives together, but they're separate.

You have this personal life that's very separated from that, but at some point, for a little bit of time say in the evening, the two come together. When we get together in the evening, for a time we talk about each other's goals and objectives and share what's happening in the professional world, and then we go off and do things that are completely detached from that part of our lives. To me, this kind of support is important and valuable. It's not important to some, but for me it is.

You're quoted in my book as saying that "Business is about networking, it's about people," would you please elaborate on this a little?

Yes, I would be happy to. Using my company's industry as an example. Anyone who thinks that they are building technology or something in isolation or in a vacuum, without regard to the people involved is making a big mistake. Because the technology or whatever it is has to be marketed and sold. You have to have people come and build it, and so it's all about getting your message out, communicating with people, motivating people...If you think about the relationships of businesses, yes, it's about profit and all of those things, but it comes together by a team of marketing people convincing someone to buy something, so it's all about relationships and people. And it's a key ingredient to making it all work.

What was the most challenging moment experienced by your enterprise thus far?

Okay. Well, you know I came out of an intrapreneurial environment, and my transition to InfoSeer was successful because customers had a problem, I understood what the need was and I knew how to differentiate my company to get that business—and when you start your own company, that's your vision—to offer something that people will be interested in buying from you. If you challenge yourself, and you decide to go after venture capital money—they don't care much about the problem. What they do care about is how much money are they going to make.

Now there's nothing wrong with this, but I would caution your readers who are new to entrepreneuring to expect this and accept it. For me, it was an unexpected experience and it was a problem for me. There was a disconnect; between the way I'm used to thinking, and when I went in to talk with these guys, I would say "We are solving this problem," and they would respond: "We don't care. How much money will this make, and when are we going to make it?"

So they were pushing on things that to me were incongruent with "We are trying to solve a problem that's really important." Therefore I'd advise your readers to think carefully about how they present their business venture, *and to keep in mind that a VC's singular focus is on making money—and to be okay with this.*

Great advice. You have to understand what's important to the various stakeholders in your business. What's meaningful to one isn't for another.

Exactly.

What was one of your most surprising moments?

A nice, pleasant surprise is that, despite all the course corrections we've had to make, we are well positioned in the market space. Probably the most rewarding thing is that now a lot of customers are indicating to us that they really need what we are offering, so the vision that we set in place a couple of years ago is coming to fruition. I think this is in large part due to our ability to get some investment monies into the business and also due to our commitment to staying the course.

Staying the course. That leads in nicely to my next question. You know, it's really common for entrepreneurs to get distracted from their mission. They land this customer, or they find themselves stressed financially, maybe scrambling to meet payroll and pay the bills. How have you managed to 'manage' the distractions? I know you've gone through some of this—we all have.

That's a great question. I think, for me anyway, it was really taking the time to write a plan. You know, it's amazing to me when I talk to other entrepreneurial people, how they don't write a plan. They kind of have this 'napkin idea' and they think they are going to run off with it.

But, if you write the plan and you really do your homework, answering the tough questions like: What are my strengths and weaknesses? Where do I need to align with other partners? What is the market size, and how am I going to penetrate that market? What happens is you're able to evolve with all the changes as everything ebbs and flows around you.

If you have a course, and all kinds of things are going to come at you: you're going to be rained on, blessed with sudden unexpected business—all kinds of things, but if you know where you are going it's just part of the process and you can get through it. And so I would say that is something that was incredibly valuable to us.

Yes. The planning forces you to ask yourself the tough questions, and really understand what the business is.

Yes, it really does. And while I wouldn't recommend the 'encyclopedia' version, it really takes you through a due diligence process: Is this market right? Are we right?

Do we know what we are doing...

Do we know what we are doing? Right. Who else is out there? Who can encroach on our space?

Well...Based on everything that we've talked about and everything that you've gone through and are going through, is there any other words of wisdom that you would like to pass on to the readers?

I'd have to say that perseverance is really important.: Persevere, persevere, persevere—never lose your vision, never give up. All of the doors you want access may not instantly open for you. Venturing is a process that is a gradual process that makes it all come together. If you are pursuing something that you know is powerful and you understand the market, stay the course in that market. Don't allow advisors, and external people to say "Well, why don't you do something over in this market?" A market where you have absolutely no knowledge and have no experience in. Because what happens is you get pulled into a direction that you may not know, and it seems great at the time, but you don't have enough market knowledge to carry your enterprise forward there.

So as an entrepreneurial person, you really want to be able to say: "I understand my business and the market I'm playing in." For me, I'd really recommend that you play in the market you know best or have the most interest in first, then explore others…

Nancy, this was great information—very powerful. Thank you.

Chris, your welcome. It was fun. You're doing a great thing putting this book out.

Thanks

In Summary:

As you can see from the information covered in this chapter, the building stage of any endeavor is extremely dense. It is the first of two very critical stages, the second being growth. Really give thought to the discussion that Akhil and Nancy have shared with you. By taking the time to really think, to consider some of the advice they've shared, you could very well save yourself many years and thousand's of dollars worth of wrong turns and bad decisions.

I know the material is getting to be a bit dense, but read through it. The information you are getting could very well be the key ingredient that helps crystallize your thinking and catapults your business to the level of success that you're striving for.

For you veterans out there—you benefit from seeing the different choices your peers have taken, and hopefully it provides inspiration for you as well.

Let's keep going, shall we?

There's a lot that goes on in this stage, and it seems to involve everything at once.

If we look at the business development model again, you will see that both Akhil and Nancy touched on every level in this model:

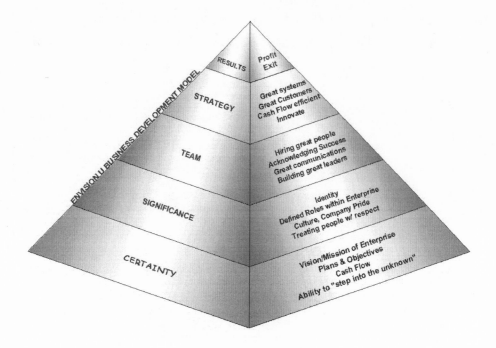

In the Building phase of the enterprise, questions you may want to consider include:

Which market or markets are we best suited to play in? What's it going to take to succeed in it? Who are the key players in this market? Can our board help us?

Do we have the right people and basic systems in place? Have we established our business identity?

Do we really know our customers? How do we treat them as partners? Do we need to align my business with others to serve them?

Does my business require capital investment or can we bootstrap it by reinvesting cash (revenue)? If we go the outside funding route, is our growth and market potential big enough to interest venture capitalist, or should we consider angel investors?

Do I know enough about my business, the markets we are in, or do I need to find expertise to tap?

CHAPTER VI

The Business Manager:
Growing the Enterprise

"... Try to make people happy, and you lay the groundwork for misery. Try to make people moral, and you lay the groundwork for vice.
Thus the Master is content to serve as an example and not to impose her will.
She is pointed, but doesn't pierce. Straightforward, but supple. Radiant, but easy on the eyes." -~ Lao-tzu

Okay, so the enterprise has survived the chaos and crisis that occurs during launch (or in the case of you veterans out there—expansion). The leaders of the enterprise have successfully steered clear of dead-ends. Money's been found, either through revenues, or angel funding or capital investment. And customers…Ah, the customers. The business has them, and is generating profit by serving them. The plan is being executed and the Builder entrepreneur, though a little battle weary, has a smile on their face, knowing that we've made it, that we've survived the rough seas and are still standing!

You should absolutely congratulate yourself for getting here. How do you know you've arrived at this phase? You can *easily* pay your bills, meet payroll, and if you look around, you may begin to notice all the people that somewhere along the way you've hired, and people are still coming in the door. They, like the rest of the world, sense that the business is viable, and they want to play.

Friends call in amazement: Wow! You survived! Amazing—let's have lunch. Better yet, I want to work for you! Always knew you'd make it!

The Growth stage is *very interesting*. Architects, and Builder types suddenly find themselves having to manage more, manage everything all at once it seems.

It's a different kind of excitement, of momentum. Now, you have companies interested in partnering, you have customers who've grown confident in your business and they want certain things too. Everyone wants "just a few minutes" of your time to discuss something—time you no longer have.

Suddenly, you're delegating your head off. You start using words like "gatekeeper," and it's quite possible you don't answer emails anymore—and your cell phone number has changed...

...Am I getting warm?

Yes, some of this was supposed to be funny. Hilarious even. If it wasn't—then re-read the last few paragraphs. If you are still not laughing—then you are definitely in the midst of growth phase—and you need to find some way to laugh in this stage.

Growth will eat you alive if you do not strike a balance between fulfilling your needs as well as the business.

Entrepreneurs of all types, employees at every level, need to be very careful while working in a business that's running in hyper-time. *The business has infinite needs,* and it will take everything you have to give it. Discipline, having a plan, knowing what the strategies are for running the business and sticking to your rules are VITAL in this stage.

It's an exciting time, because for the first time, everyone can actually see evidence of the vision, the outcome that the leaders kept talking about some time ago. Possibilities say a year ago, are now tangible realities.

What I hear over and over again from entrepreneurs who are operating in this phase is: "Things move *fast* here." While it's true, you are tested at every phase of the business cycle; it's in the Growth phase that you find out if the business model and its systems work. Here, they either work or break. Any short cuts you might have chosen in the past, or systems you neglected to build, haunt you in the growth stage.

Opportunity, and customer demand is at an all-time high, wealth finally occurs or is within site by investors, founders, key employees—everything is very big, very real and very, very rapid moving...

At this phase, the company has the highest probability to succeed, however it's also at this stage that the original founders experience the most pressure. Any weaknesses they may have in terms of knowledge, expertise or managerial competence is greatly magnified here. It's not uncommon to find that the original founders begin to seek out to augment or even replace the company's management team. They correctly note that the venture has new needs in terms of organizational resources, and they either stretch to meet these needs or seek out resources to meet them.

The majority of small businesses purchased in this country occur during the building and growth stages, largely due to a company's founders disinterest in continuing to operate the company.

But the readers of this book have an edge. You've built your enterprise correctly, invested in the right systems and resources, and you've created the teams necessary to thrive in all stages.

A great example of a Master Entrepreneur who's thriving in this stage is Art Sands of AC Technology, Inc. (www.actechnology.com). I met Art last year while competing in a billiards league of all places. Like in golf, it's a small world, and you get to know people beyond the sport-and Art was no exception. We ended up talking about what we did for a living, and the rest is history.

I have to tell you: Art Sands is one of the wisest businessmen I've run across. Of course, I gave him the third degree, asking questions, trying to find the weakness and vulnerabilities to his business model and strategy...where one should have expected to find a dozen minor and major issues, I found only one-and it is minor indeed. Art's an interesting example for the readers of this book because he's started a business before, has transitioned the business to the company that it is today, and has thrived in dealing with the most complex of customers-The U.S. Government.

And he's an intelligent risk-taker, and has bet the company on more than one occasion in taking it to a new direction or another level-and won the hand. Art is one-half of a dynamic duo. His other partner is his brother, and by all accounts this partnership is a raving success. Well, let me have him tell the story…

Note: This interview was four hours in duration. In the coming months, I will post the full interviews on the site (www.visualcv.com/wealthdna). Email me at **Wealthdna@gmail.com** and request to be put on my mailing list. You'll be notified once information is posted.

Basically I want to ask you a few questions, hitting on six key areas. I want to start with basically the company overview, just get a little background information, and then the next categories would be questions regarding risk taking, integrity, hiring great employees, pursuing the opportunities, taking chances and strategy in partnerships and the like (?). So, those are the areas that I wanted to touch on today.

OK

Let's go ahead and get started. So basically, in your own words, can you tell me what is AC technology? I know the company has gone through a lot of changes.

Yes, we've been through a number of changes, and actually it's really helped us to be able to move on opportunities just prior to major technology shifts, but we started out as a… I guess you'd call a storage management company, and what we did was we built drivers for mass storage devices to be attached to the Unix platform, basically Sun Microsystems, because Sun really had no storage in 1991 to speak of and there was a lot of play in the large, near-time storage, or just off-line…near-line, off-line and so on. And so large jukeboxes, large tape systems, large disk systems.

Sun Microsystems really didn't have anything that met the needs so we built drivers specifically for large-scale storage. And then as those scsi 3 and scsi 2 started to come out, and there was more and more…you know, and raid disk storage was starting to become more and more prominent, we decided right then and there …we saw this happening and we knew that the days of the driver were over.

So, we started to branch out, and the first thing that we did was we added Oracle, Cisco and Veritas to our service offering…so that we complete…not only keep our storage management background intact, but also develop in ways that would give us a wider customer base.

By the mid 1990's we had pretty much moved from being primarily a storage management and integration company into data center integration, and so we did it all. We put in the Oracle, we put in the storage management, we did the storage, and even if they didn't buy it from us, we were there to help with professional services to go in and integrate all this stuff. And then, we…I guess 4.5 years ago, we moved into…well, lets say 6 years ago, we started to move into data security.

We were seeing that the internet...the constant barrage of news about, this virus breaks in here and that virus breaks in there, and so we were...we saw that security was going to play a very large role, not only on the internet, but on the data from inside the company as well. So, we started with Cisco and the name of their product was called CiscoPix and we started there with data security and gradually started to branch out into things like database encryption, although we didn't really sell anything, we just started investigating that.

And then we were looking at logical access. And after we did about 2 years of research, about 4 years ago or 4.5 years ago, we saw that access to data was going to become, or at least we felt that it would be, important and that the username and password scenarios were just not working. So, they had PKI (public key infrastructure; a security protocol) and that's all well and good, but it's still just a number. It's still something that...PKI is just...I just saw that it was changing. So, we sat down and we said, "you know, the one way that you can identify yourself that says that you are who you are, truly, is biometrics."

And so we started to work in biometrics and pattern recognition, and we actually started with facial recognition and then realized that it would be a long haul for facial. And so we turned our efforts towards using things like fingerprint and voice and iris and there are other signature recognition. There's a whole host of different types of biometrics, and also data encryption on the network side and on the database side.

When you say "a long haul in the facial recognition" what do you mean by that?

Well, facial recognition is still...I mean, there were a lot of early pretenders to the throne. And they caused more damage to the biometrics industry that they helped the biometrics industry.

How did you recognize that? How were you able to avoid that?

First of all, we knew that most of the systems...this is the way we felt: we knew that all of the systems today were Microsoft. There were no Unix solutions. And the other thing was that everybody was building biometric solutions out of pure software. It was pure software play in facial recognition. And anybody knows that the larger the database gets, the slower the performance will be in a pure software environment. So we decided that we would look for research and development that was either ongoing or something that we could start where they were going to combine both hardware and software.

They'd need to have some kind of ancillary computer of some kind that would do the pre-processing and the pre-sorting so that you don't drag down the system. And that's when we sold the 64-bit PCI card as a medium, and we started the project.

Sun was extremely helpful in the beginning because they gave us close to $1,000,000 in funding to go after this, and that's plus our own funds as well. They paid for a portion of this. And so, they were extremely interested because we were going to develop on their Sun Solaris platform first, and we were going to build a PCI card that ran on their machines.

So Sun Microsystems had a lot of vested interest.

Right, so there was a lot of interest in facial recognition, they're always looking for solutions. And we wrote a business plan and showed them what we were going to do, how long the research would, and they agreed to assist us. As a result, in March of 2004, we issued our first release of the facial recognition system.

Wow, congratulations.

Thank you. It's been a 4 -1/2 year effort...sometimes you just look at it and say, "Am I just tossing stuff down a rat hole? Am I becoming a victim of my own hype, or is something really going to take off?" Because I know facial recognition is long and strong in the eyes of the intelligence community. And we started in facial recognition long before 9/11. We also started data access control; authenticated data access control well before 9/11, so...

To answer you question about throwing money down a rat hole, I have to answer it with this comment: how do I buy shares in your company?

I expect that the first release of the facial recognition software, as with all first releases, will require some re-tooling to optimize to take advantage of new technology. But that's the nature of the business-constant and never-ending improvements...

And now, there are agencies within the government that are interested in pursuing further development of the facial recognition technology. And again, that's good for us, because it's not coming out of my pocket and I don't have to give up a stake in the product or share the intellectual property rights...

That's excellent.

I'm looking forward to this part of it. So now, we have really two divisions: one is biometrics research and development and products, and the other is the same systems integration business along with, I guess you'd call it web-based information sharing, because that's really all of Sun's new products. You know it started with NetScape and then iPlanet and then SunOne and now Java Enterprise System. Well, we've been in that for I don't know how many years.

Regarding risk taking, I believe that every successful entrepreneur is enduring significant crises and challenges or other events. At that point the entrepreneur usually has to make a decision, take the next step or not. What would you say is AC technologies defining moment, if you can point to one?

If I could point to one...

Yes. You know the scenario. The business is faced with a major turning point and it's the 11th hour...

I think launching into research and development early on in biometrics was a major risk because we actually...if they give you a contract you can build it...we actually...if you build it, they will come.

And that was a major risk on our part. It was at the urging of Sun, but certainly with not all of their backing. Do you know what I mean? I mean, they didn't fund the entire project, and it required a major investment on our part in this technology, and it has vaulted AC Technology, not only in terms of it's professional services, but by putting us in the public eye, people realize how much we went through to get where we are.

I mean, we've sustained 40% growth over 13 years of business, every year. That's our average. And we made the VAR 500 last year and the VAR fast 50, from VAR business. We were number 36 in the VAR fast 50 and number 444 out of the VAR 500. That's a lot for a 20% company. The whole thing is…and our reputation is…we have a lot of certifications, most of my engineers, all of my engineers are core certified in Solaris, but the major thing is the ancillary certifications, the storage, the web based information sharing certifications, the things like citirx and tarantella, fatwire, all these different things that all come together to allow us to provide the maximum benefit for web based or network based information sharing. That means the technology, the security and the delivery.

You have to be able to do it all. At least, we believe that. And even though we're small, our professional services group is growing, and I'll be adding a lot more people this year.

So you have certified competency throughout the entire service chain?

Yes. We have to have competency…sometimes the training isn't mandatory, but it is in my company. Because we won't see what we don't know. And we're very, very picky about the products that we bring on-line and we also make sure that all the engineers and the sales people are thoroughly trained in that so that when they speak, they speak with some knowledge and now just, "let me get back to you." So, education is a key factor here and all of our engineers are encouraged…it's not like, they can not go to this class. It's like, go to this class, submit the form, it'll be approved, especially if we know it's core technology.

Wow, that's amazing. So, that was pretty much the defining moment?

Yes, I would say that our launch into research and development in the area of biometric access control was a defining moment for AC because the publicity that it got us and the traction within the major vendors that we represent, vaulted us to them giving us more business because they realize that these guys know Java programming, they know…I mean, this is a very, very technically competent company. These guys work hard here.

So, were there any other times where you found yourselves having to take really extraordinary risks?

We're also pretty much a Sun shop, and committing to a single vendor, we were multi-vendor before, but we realized that we'll never be able to certify enough engineers to cover everybody and be able to do…because the money is not in the hardware. Everybody knows that. It's in the software and services, so for us, we said we have to choose a vendor and we chose the most open system on the market and we decided to build our solutions around Sun first, and whenever possible build into Java.

And that just gave us a multi-platform environment for our own software, but provided us with...I mean the loyalty we had shown Sun has come back to us with their investment in our company. So, I could have been a vendor for everybody and just priced delivery, but you would really have to be huge to make any margin doing that, to make a profit.

And so, the fact that we chose to be a single vendor point of focus and focus around solutions that attach to that, very important, and it was a very big step for us because we said, "we're going to give up these other lines. We're not going to sell this anymore. We're going to dedicate ourselves, we're going to certify ourselves and become experts at Solaris, Java and the Sun server environment." And that's exactly what we did. We're enterprise-partner with Sun, we're storage-partner with Sun, and we're Java enterprise system-partner with Sun.

In the book I say that the Master Entrepreneur operates from a very high level of integrity and competence, and that they are unwavering in their character. I happen to know you personally, and that you're someone who operates this way, and you demand the same in return. In your opinion, do you feel this gives your company an edge? And if so, in what way?

Well, I'll tell you, coming up through a lot of people saying, "Trust me," or, "I give you my word." And it takes a while for people to believe you because nobody wants to take you at your word. So, in the 13 years that we've been in business, our customers and vendors alike know that when we talk to them, we're honest with them. We're straight up. If we think something is wrong, we don't hesitate to tell them, "This is a problem and you need to fix it, or it's only going to get worse."

Or, if I tell a customer, "I'm going to fix this problem for you." Then, if I have to come out of pocket to fix it, the most important thing that you have...the technology is all there...the most important thing that you have, especially with a customer to gain their trust...because you have thousands of people out there like us. Bigger companies than us, much larger, and they have...but if I give you my word that I'm going to do something and I do it, that carries a lot of weight with the end user customer, and they will come back again and again knowing that you will perform exactly what you say you will do.

When I say it's going to be ready on Thursday, then it's ready on Thursday if we have to work all night. If I say I'm going to complete this project for you no matter what, then we do it. And if we have to come out of pocket, then we come out of pocket because your word is all you have.

That's right.

That's all you have... Your reputation in business is everything, especially when you're a small company. Your reputation is everything. One mistake...that could ruin you.

We've talked on a couple of occasions about the quality of the customer. Do you believe that it makes a difference as to whether a company thrives or simply survives? And do you believe that taking on the wrong customer can sink the business?

Oh, yes. If you take on the wrong customer...For instance, just look at WinStar. We were WinStar's data center integrator. We did a lot of work with WinStar, we were doing over a million dollars a month. And, Chris

(Art's Brother and CEO of AC Technology) had the foresight when he looked into their financials...because WinStar is spending a lot of money...and he started to hear rumblings in the street about WinStar and the fact that their broadband was...there's a lot of hype, but very little performance and so we start seeing this stuff in the trade magazines and so he started to...we bought a share of stock each and then we started looking at the financial reports and things like that, and all of the sudden he's looking at it and he's going, "we can't give these guys any more credit."

So, that's what he did. So, we pulled their credit and they had to pay cash on delivery. Well, the only time they would use us then is if they had do, that they couldn't get any more credit from somebody else. They sunk two companies in the process. One lost $2.6 million, the other lost $4.1 million. Both had to sell their companies to other people.

A lot of companies got hurt with WinStar. One of the companies I was consulting for, Metro IS, a recruiting company, saw $1.5 million in receivables just vaporized.

See, that's the thing: if you put all your eggs into that one basket, especially with commercial companies, they can change on a whim. If you have a relationship with the Director of Engineering and all of a sudden someone else has a relationship with the CTO or the CIO, all of a sudden you find yourself...what did I do wrong? I didn't do anything wrong.

Well, you weren't high enough in the food chain. If other people can make decisions that negate your customer service, then you're finished. And for us, that's why we chose to start with government.

Our commercial clients are very few, but now that we're ready...we're a solid, stable company. We have no debt. So, now we're going to launch into assisting the oil companies with their security needs, and we're going to take it one step at a time.

Sounds like a good plan...

We're not going to go crazy here and take on too much business because otherwise what happens is, they look at you and you're responsible. One thing happens, you're out. So that big $20 million-dollar contract, or that big $10 million-dollar contract vaporizes overnight, then you have to dump your infrastructure and re-tool everything. And then your reputation suffers, because that becomes big news out on the street...

And then it's de-motivating. It hurts everything, the culture.

It hurts everybody to lose out like that and so we're very, very cautious. Which is why it's 13 years, but our growth has been steady and I would say conservatively paced. Even though we've had 40% growth every year, its...our average is 40% over the 13 year period, the whole thing is that we've really managed that growth so that we can handle everything we take on. I'm the first one to admit,

I'll hire consultants to go in and do something, especially if I can't do it myself, or if my engineers are busy, I look for qualified personnel to augment my own, to go in there and assist with certain problems, or challenges, whatever you want to call them. I prefer challenges. But you hire experts as you need them, but you don't throw all your money into overhead if there aren't sustaining contracts that are 150% of what you're doing.

So, in other words, I want that guy off the bench. I don't want him sitting there collecting a paycheck and working 80% of the time. I want him booked 150% of the time so that he's moving and I have to bring in ancillary help just to cover the extra hours. That's the way we try to do it here. We run a very lean shop. That's why we didn't fall by the wayside like many others.
Because you had an excess of demand on the books?

Yes. We keep the ratio stacked in favor of excess demand...we want the people who have been with us all this time to benefit. So, if I grow my infrastructure that means I have to spread the same customer base over a larger group and go after new customers. Well, nothing consumes dollars more than chasing new customers.

It's so true. The most lucrative customer is the one you've already landed.

Yep. You may win when you get a new customer, but you have to chase them to get them. So when we chase, we go after a very specific target where we really think we have a better than 75% chance of getting that client, otherwise it's just not worth it to us to do that. We have plenty of clients base to work with. So, we're getting ready to expand now into the commercial sector. We have a couple of commercial contracts, but for the most part we're government.

Okay. It's really great that two brothers are able to work together in a business like this.

Yes, Chris and I have been together since 1974.

How are you complementing one another? What roles do you take on for one another?

(Laughter) Well, Chris is Mr. No and I'm Mr. Yes.

Really? He's the hammer, huh?

Yes, he is the President and CEO, and he handles administration and finance. He is truly the CFO of the company and the guy that really has kept AC's reputation and creditworthiness and the fact that we have no debt. That's all him. I'm the COO. I handle the operations and explore the deal-making opportunities between customers, partners and the like.

It sounds like you both are involved with the strategy.

Yes, of course, if you're going to be partners you have to work together. I do operations, so I cover engineering and sales. And I'm responsible for the professional services organization, their training and everything else. Now, I have a Director of Business Development and then there are a number of sales people. And I have a Director of Engineering and the engineers under him, but all in all, Chris runs administration and finance and I run the sales and engineering.

And that's my forte. I did the same thing in the other company we had before it was acquired by McDonald Douglas: he was finance and I was operations and it worked very well. He has a strong grip-- I'm not a finance person.

In this setup, you don't have to be.

We sit down and we bounce things off each other and even though sometimes we may disagree, ultimately, one of us says to the other, OK, let's go with it, we'll go with your idea. So, it's not something where we're always juxtaposed. You have to make a decision, you have to say OK, am I making this decision because I personally feel this, or am I making a good business decision?

We both offer support for our ideas and then either I convince him, or he convinces me. And that's the way we operate. It's been a great partnership that way. Plus when it's your brother you have your best interests at heart all the time. So we complement each other very well. We're both very outgoing, so we're good representatives for our company and we know how to complement each other in meetings and things like that. If he has a question that he feels I can answer better than him, then he just hands it over to me.

And a lot of meetings we don't attend together because we just only have so much time, but we know and we trust each other to say the right thing and do the right thing and not make a decision too early without consulting the other. We don't do that. We don't make just a decision out of hand. We build all the information together, then we sit down and discuss it, then we say OK, this is the way we should go.

It works so well. It's really kept us moving…you can tell that atmosphere is the same with all the employees. We don't have the traditional problems that sales and engineering has.

There's usually a lot of conflict between sales and every other division of a company.

Sales people think they make all the money and the engineers say, "Well, you couldn't make all that money if we didn't make it all work."

Right.

In many companies there's real rivalry between sales and engineers. Every sales person goes out with an engineer. They work together. Everybody gets compensation for that. Everybody gets a bonus for brining in new business. Everybody – from the administrative staff to the engineers to the sales people.

Everybody gets something. This way everybody feel like they're a part of every deal we do. And that to me is what builds...I mean, all these people here, except some new people, they've been with me 8 years or more. And that's a long time to stay with a small company.

Yes, especially with all the changes you've put it through.

And Jerry Timpton, our Director of Business Development, he says, "Art, let me tell you something. Everybody can make you a promise. But all I know is I've never had a payroll missed, I never lost a commission, I've never been refused a single accommodation here. Why in the hell would I want to leave? Everyone can promise you more money, and then 6 months down the road, when they feel that maybe your position has cost them too much, they terminate you. Here I know I make a difference. That means more to me than just a little extra cash."

I have to write another book, and it's on your company! This is textbook. This is how it should be done. A lot of your employees, do they come to you from referrals?

From other employees?

Yes.

Yes, and from people who say, "I know this person." And we interview them, we talk to them and this is very...I don't want to say mercurial because that would sound like we're just running on...We have a very high intensity level here. So when you interview employees, it's not just their capabilities, but can they thrive in this atmosphere. Will the rest of my employees get along with this person? And sometimes the answer is no. No matter how good they look, you have to be able to judge, will they become a part of this team or are they too big company? That's why I have a hard time hiring people from places like Sun. I have a lot of people that would love to work here, but they all come from big company mentality.

Yes, they can't move fast enough.

And it takes a strong readjustment to do that. It can be a strong readjustment...

And you have to play team there. You have to check the ego at the door...

That's why when the interview process takes place it's not just me, it's the sales guy, the engineering guy, the VP for administration. We make them a part of the interview process because it's important that everybody have an input into knowing what do you think of this person? Do you think they would thrive here? Because you don't want somebody to come to work for you and then after 90 days say this isn't what I wanted, and leave.

Yes, it's devastating.

Rather than waste my time and theirs, I'd rather pre-qualify them here. And even if we make a mistake, well, we made a mistake. We should have hired that person, but we didn't. Well, OK. But, better that way than to bring somebody in who we know isn't going to work out.

You know, I was really impressed how you pursued this guy, I think from Holland, this developer...a "must hire" as your key developer put it...was it Holland?

It was Finland.

Finland, thank you. One of your key resources said, "Art, I have to have this guy." And I was just really impressed with how you went after this guy. You took a chance in terms of...

...there was definitely some risk. My lead developer flatly told me that this was the guy to help us get the code where it had to be. He said, "I need this person because I may be able to think it up, but he's the guy who could implement it, build the code, actually execute." "This is the guy that I would bring onto this project." So, I said, "OK, let's bring him on." And it turned out to exceed my expectations.

What compelled you to make that extra effort to meet this request?

First of all, you can't really develop a product with a single person, even if they are the designer, creator...no one person can do everything, no matter how brilliant they are.

Well, we had heard about this team programming concept. IBM was doing it long ago, where they put two people together. It's called extreme programming. And what they end up doing is, two people working together actually can do more than four people working alone. And because they're so in tune with one another and the way they work and things like that, that even though the design concept may come from one side of the rough code, he already knows where the guy is going with this and then starts to optimize what he does to make that guy's vision a reality.

And these two guys complement each other so well, that they produce more stuff in less time than if I had four guys working on it that were all working individually.

For me, Art Sands and his company represent the best in what small business can mean.

CHAPTER VII

The Business Integrator:

Building a Great Collection of Companies

"... The Master lets all things come and go effortlessly, without desire. She never expects results; thus she is never disappointed. She is never disappointed; thus her spirit never grows old."

—Lao-tzu

For some of you, getting to this stage is true victory for you. Any one of the three types of Entrepreneurs can become Integrators—they just have to have a winning formula, one that makes them want to do it all over again.

Mad scientists, inventors, chefs and entrepreneurs have this in common: All are seeking the perfect formula to achieve their outcomes.

Entrepreneurs who've taken their business from concept to growth and beyond, and who want to do it all over again, become integrators.

Some set out to build large businesses in the first place. Building businesses through acquiring existing business is an old tried and true formula, executed successfully by the likes of Rockefeller, Getty and Carnegie. Some modern day examples include Rupert Murdoch, and Oprah Winfrey.

There are several situations that could cause a Master Entrepreneur to become an Integrator. Sometimes, it can occur out of necessity, meaning the enterprise has succeeded to such a degree that acquisitions become necessary to sustain its success. It can occur as a result of new business interest found in a completely different market or industry, but in every case, an entrepreneur's previous successes are brought to bear on integration activities. And it can occur as a result of public demand, bringing you an opportunity to do it all over again.

This translates to recreating teams, systems, and recycling strategies that worked in an old venture and applying them to a new one.

In the case of Nancy Curtis, for example, she took the experience and knowledge she gained from building a billion-dollar division for her employer and recycled those skills into creating InfoSeer, which ironically enough, is destined to become a billion-dollar enterprise.

Becoming an Integrator Entrepreneur largely occurs as a happy and unintended result of achieving extraordinary success in your ventures. In terms of the enterprise life cycle:

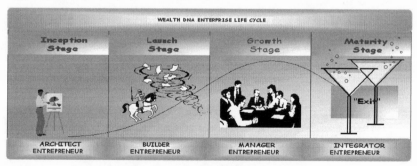

Integration activities occur largely in the maturity phases of a business. With regard to technology, research, patents and the like, acquisition can occur at any time, but acquiring businesses *with the intent of keeping them largely intact* generally occurs at the maturity phase.

An amazing example of a Master Entrepreneur who's thriving in this stage is Aslan Mirkalami, CEO of Rugman.com, Inc. (www.rugman.com). I've had the pleasure of getting to know Aslan through Envision U's WealthBuilders Program- he is one of the program's role models. Envision U recently had the honor of working with him to transition his enterprise to reach the 100-million dollar revenue level.

In some ways, it is easier to be an entre/intrapreneur at this level— there is an abundance of resources, strategies, and experiences from which one can drawn upon to succeed here. And in other ways, it is profoundly more difficult to operate at this level, as little mistakes in judgment can have a huge impact on the overall success of the enterprise.

Integrators such as Aslan, with one decision can generate tremendous wealth. They are constantly generating, assessing and acting on ideas and taking risks, and due to their previous string of successes, (or as in the case of Aslan's friend: failures) operate with an extraordinary high level of confidence and certainty.

Integrators win a lot and lose often, but at the end of the day, they enjoy more wins, because at this level, experiencing success is a habit.

Aslan's psychology regarding both wealth and entrepreneuring is nothing short of extraordinary. The wisdom that he has runs deep, and I hope you gain a lot from the following interview.

Aslan, I want to thank you for making time for this interview. I'm grateful that you've found time in your travel schedule to do this.

You're quite welcome. Anything I can do to support you. Let's go.

Okay. What would you say is the single most important character trait that a entrepreneur must have if he or she is to be successful?

The most important characteristic that an entrepreneur must have is a lack of fear. I can't speak for everyone, but I know that it has been a major factor in my own success. Let me give you what I think would make someone very successful and then we will start ranking them, okay?

Great, let's do it.

I think what makes me really successful is number one: I'm not afraid. I'm not afraid of failing, I'm not afraid of trying. In fact, what I say to my assistant I come up with 100 ideas a day; I know 99 of them are not going to be any good. I know 90 of them would be junk. I know 9 would be impossible to do, but I know 1 of that 100 is going to be a life-changing experience. So what I want is to be able to sift through and try—we won't be able to find out which ideas are brilliant unless you actually go and look, and that takes a certain level of bravery.

Let me give you an example: I have a friend, he is a multi multi-millionaire, in fact he was recently offered 100 million dollars for his company (which he declined.) He's worth well over several hundred million dollars. At one time, he had hit a dry spell; he was trying new things, and one of his worst failures involved experimenting with creating a vendor franchising system involving corn. But the thing is, he was brave enough to go in the face of adversity and the disbelief of everyone who worked for me, and force them, or convince them to try this new idea.

The point is, it takes a certain amount of courage to go in the face of adversity. And everyone's opinion was that this was not a good idea; he went ahead and still did it, and though he failed miserably, he didn't give up. He tried different things, different ideas. At some point, he opened a company called Gold Mine, thinking that he was going to rent a large facility, then sub-lease smaller space to several jewelers and create a jeweler's market. Well, that didn't work either, but then he went on to pre-paid calling card system, and changed his company from Gold Mine to Gold Line, the company that he was offered 100 million for.

It was a time in his life when he was at rock bottom. He had nothing left. His house was in foreclosure, his car was reposed, and he came to me for a loan or help with negotiating with a bank for bridge financing. And basically he had a certain level of conviction that I have never seen in many other people. He was very convinced that this would work after failing maybe a hundred times, and hitting barrier after barrier. He was convinced this was the one.

So, in his darkest hour, he launched what ended up being a 100 million dollar company.

Yes. In fact I had a very good chance of owning half of it for a couple of hundred thousand dollars. But I started doubting him, because he had a string of failures for several years. So, the entrepreneur has to be brave enough to act on their ideas. Everyone has ideas, but the entrepreneur takes a step further and acts on some of them. And they are very persistent.

People were telling this guy, give up, get a job, let the bank take the home, get an apartment, but he didn't, he persisted. Eventually, he received the money he needed and he was able to grow the company, but he was nearly out. You know, time tests you. It tests you; wanting to know exactly how badly do you want a thing. How much do you really deserve to get this? In my friend's case, it to him to the brink, but it was not even four months later he was happy, and in five years he built the company to what it is today.

Amazing. Let me ask you, do you find that your friend is still taking chances, still experimenting?

Yes, to this day, he's still experimenting, trying new things. I recently introduced him to the Director for Pizza Hut in Canada, and within two days, he had struck an agreement in which, with every pizza, a free calling card would be offered. He went to a bank, and negotiated with the bank, to sell out of their ATM machines, calling cards. It's the first time anyone has made that connection. It's easier for me to talk about him than myself, but he and I are identical in this.

So, an entrepreneur has to be brave and they have to be willing to try ideas, to experiment.

It's really interesting. My friends that I've known for years, I've always told them that I was going to be an entrepreneur and write a book—they didn't believe me. It really does take persistence.

Yes, it takes a lot of persistence and a lot of bravery and creativeness. Now entrepreneurs are heavy into driving. And the reason is because they come up with ideas that everyone resists them on, so they have to be able to force people to act on them, otherwise ideas are just ideas. To me, an entrepreneur is one who focuses on getting the job done and who'll get the end result and deliver it. So, the difference between someone who has good ideas and somebody who's an entrepreneur is the entrepreneur gets it done. He's brave enough to go right through it, and take actions, whatever it takes.

My commitment, and every other entrepreneur's commitment is to reach the objective. And we are results-oriented. I'm not in love with the process; I'm in love with the result.

Right. That makes sense. Okay, in the book, I've devoted a chapter discussing financial pressure. It is the greatest test an entrepreneur faces. Even the most successful entrepreneur at one time or another is faced with financial pressure.

Yes.

Sometimes, there can be a chain of events, which result in this pressure. What advice would you give my readers who are going to find themselves facing that test even if they're not an entrepreneur?

Yes. Bend and don't break.

Okay.

It's happened to me many times. I mean, when I say it's happened many times, it's not my habit, but it's happened. And it's circumstantial; risks I've taken that didn't pay off or went against me, and I never regret it, because if I didn't take those risks I wouldn't be here.

Right.

If it wasn't in my nature to take those kinds of risks, I wouldn't have been able to create the life I now enjoy. I would be working for someone, or I would be a 9 to 5 type of guy. So when I say "Bend, don't break."

Thanks Aslan

Any time, my friend.

CHAPTER VIII:

Investors & Investment

"I believe that we are like instruments. Whether the instrument is used constructively or poorly depends on us. We have a good mind and a good heart. If we combine these two—the education of the mind and the compassion of the heart, then a contribution will be constructive... You will have the determination, optimism, patience, courage and faith to overcome all obstacles."
~ Dalai Lama

At some point along the entrepreneurial path, you will be faced with the critical decision: Do we grow the venture, or leave it as it is? And if we chose the growth path, do we or don't we take on capital (outside investment)? Here's a typical scenario: You've taken the business as far as you can go, bootstrapping (i.e. using all generate revenues and other resources, reinvested back into the business) it as far as you can. To get to the next level of business activity, you believe that the business needs an infusion of cash from some source outside of revenues.

Should we seek investment? Are we really ready to take on the responsibility of working with someone else's money? And if so, who should we approach and what's it going to cost us?

These are the typical questions most entrepreneurs face when opportunities for growth present themselves. But, like most of life's journey, there are many paths to choose from.

The Master Entrepreneur, at some point in their journey, may have to select from among several possible paths:

- Grow the Enterprise through existing revenues and bank financing (lines of credit, signature loans, etc.)
- Grow the Enterprise through strategic partnerships, joint ventures or other business-to-business relationships
- Grow the Enterprise through replication (franchising) or subsidiary/spin-offs
- Grow the Enterprise through junk-bond financing
- Grow the Enterprise through outside capital (venture capital/investment bank or angel funding)
- Grow the Enterprise through IPO (public offering)

The entrepreneur's options depend on the type of business, that business's cash flow (ability to pay the "return-on-investment" or repayment terms), and the business's size. Most entrepreneurs prefer to grow the business from revenue and bank financing, because they don't want the burden of having to take on financial partners and they don't want to "dilute" their equity. This is especially common among family-run businesses where the owners have no intention of exiting the business but rather, pass it on to the next generation.

This is fine for most businesses, but your business's industry may require you to have more flexibility, to take advantage of unexpected and sudden opportunities that come up.

The Master Entrepreneur is careful with the business's cash, and they pursue capital based on the needs and objectives of the enterprise. If it means significant market share, they have no problems diluting equity to reap the benefits and gains in revenue being fully capitalized gives their business.

Most will *delay* seeking outside capital until the later stages of the enterprise (Growth and Maturity), as capital is at the lowest cost at these stages.

The most expensive money is at the earliest stages of the enterprise. Investors at these stages are investing in a good, but unproven idea, venture and business team (you and your team), therefore they exact the greatest % of equity and ROI (return on investment). I have heard in some cases investors demanding (and sadly, getting) as much as 75% equity of somebody's business. The younger the enterprise, the higher the cost of investment: friends and family, credit cards, angel investors and VC firms.

My advice would be to tough it out until after the startup phase, after the business has "proven itself," meaning its generating revenues, has positive cash-flow (more cash coming in than going out), customers—and is faced with growth. The longer you can delay going after outside investment, the *cheaper* that investment will ultimately cost you and you will have more leverage to create better, more tolerable terms for the transaction.

In my opinion, the majority of entrepreneurs do not explore strategic partnering enough. It is a very economical and at times fast way of gaining real increases in business growth and wealth without having to finance it.

Most, approach strategic partnerships and alliances from purely a sales or marketing gain, meaning Company A aggress to sell and market Company B's products/services, and visa versa. This is a typical agreement. But what if Company A was "rich" in sales and marketing resources (money, systems, people, channels, relationships) and Company B was rich in research and development, product branding, patent and trademarking and service fulfillment?

In this scenario, it might make a lot of sense for Company's A & B to co-develop a product or service offering together, then let each of the company's take responsibility for what they are strongest at. So, Company B researches, develops, patents (jointly) and brands their co-product and then Company A takes over and markets and sells the thing. In this case their overall investment was kept at a minimum, while at the same time they enjoy maximum gain.

Finding the right partners can be a bit challenging, but I strongly recommend you make the effort: partnering to strengths and for the right outcomes (results) can be more powerful than pure capital.

In addition, if the partnerships' outcomes are large enough, you may find that you can still attract outside investment in the joint venture itself, whereas by yourselves you wouldn't want or can't attract fairly priced capital, but together through the joint venture it makes sense.

There are an infinite number of reasons why you would or would not seek outside funding, but for those of you who feel that you are in the position of needing or believe you would benefit from outside investment, let's delve into it.

Before we go on, let me summarize a few key points:

- In general, *capital-intensive* businesses (businesses requiring large investments in plant, raw materials and equipment) usually require capitalization.
- In general, *non-capital-intensive businesses* (i.e. service businesses) do not require capitalization and therefore can be sustained from reinvestment of revenues and other resources ("bootstrapping;" cash flow)
- The cost of capital is highest for a business that's young or in decay (dying market).
- The cost of capital is lowest for a business that's mature or proven.
- Strategic alliances/joint ventures are often an overlooked and underutilized means of increases business wealth ("value")

Investors

In deciding whether or not to seek outside funding, you must determine how capital-intensive your business is, and whether it is substantial enough to justify outside investment at all. As a rule, you should only consider venture capitalization only if you intend to grow the business.

In some cases, it may prove to be unwise to grow your business. Business expansion through capitalization may actually result in less overall profitability, especially if you chose to grow through acquisition, so you must approach growth with extreme care. Eroding profitability and dilution of equity can be a bitter pill. Remember, one of the attributes of a superior enterprise is *"It is a business which can grow and be grown for the right reasons."*

Again, depending on the type of business you're in, and the market that business is playing in, you may not have a choice: you may be forced to grow to survive in the market, especially if you are in the early stages of business development. If your business is a fully mature business, you may still require outside capital for growth. Some typical reasons include:

- Changes in technology common in your industry require larger capital expenditures that can't easily be financed with cash flow and normal bank financing.
- You want to exit the business through a private sale, but without significant growth history, the sales price would not meet your requirements.
- You want to grow your company to reap the advantages your larger competitors are enjoying in terms of pricing power and efficiencies.
- Your company's competitors are eroding your market share by financing their growth with outside capital.
- To maintain or even increase market share or dominance you want to rapid-develop new products or services, but you don't want to risk existing cash flow or normal bank debt to do so.

These and dozens of other reasons would justify growing your business. For most investors, one of the top questions they will want answered is "What is the reason for growing the business? What is the motivation for doing so?" To meet payroll or to be able to provide jobs for friends and family isn't a good reason.

As you consider outside capital, ask yourself this question: "Will this investment result in significant increases in revenues, sufficient to be worth it to me and the investor(s)?" Make certain that the answer is "Yes," otherwise dig deeper in your planning and strategy until it's Yes. The return has to be there for everyone for it to be worthwhile.

About two years ago, I received a priceless lesson regarding investing. Two years ago, I was developing another enterprise based in Atlanta, Georgia. It was an engineering and construction company, and the firm was focused on the FAA market. Anyway, my partners and I decided to seek outside capital (seed capital) to use for funding the cash flow requirements on two FAA contracts the firm was awarded. The terms offered an 18-month ROI of 175% of principal, which we felt was very generous. We had about ten times principal in won contracts on our books, so we knew the downside risk was very low for the investor.

Well, we submitted our proposal. We had a sound, experienced management team, were awarded federal contracts on the books, had complete financial information, referrals, and had contingency plans for ROI. We only made one mistake—we did not do our "homework" regarding the investor! It turns out that this particular individual, while he did have a history of investing in construction plays like ours, as a rule, he never goes into these investments alone.

For this type of investment, he only investment as a part of a group, so his response to us was "Interesting proposition. From your contract wins, I'm confident in you as an entity, but this deal is too small. Come see me when you have a deal requiring investment in the five to ten million dollar range—I have friends who would be happy to invest."

Missing the little details like this can be devastating. No one thought to ask about his investment preferences. We now know that most investors have both preferences and patterns in terms of what they look like, how they invest, how they determine and manage risk.

So I would say to you: Do your homework. As diligent as you are in preparing your deal, make certain you do your research on the investors, or investor group prior to submitting.

> After the dot.com craze, and the loss of over four trillion dollars in stock market capitalization, entrepreneurs the world over have suddenly found it difficult to acquire investment capital. I believe this is only partially true.

> **Real investors** are *always investing*, always looking for opportunities to invest in. While it's true that getting to them, and having the right opportunity for them to consider may be more difficult and challenging, they are still investors and are always willing to invest *in the right opportunities.*

This has always been true, even during the go-go years of the dot com craze.

So, if it is true, what does a Master Entrepreneur need to convey or do to attract and acquire funds from an investor? Well, the very first step is you have to understand *that you are the first Investor.* Perhaps entrepreneurs work too hard at their business for too long.

Maybe they simply never saw themselves as bona fide investors in the first place, but make no mistake:

YOU ARE AN INVESTOR.

You are an early investor, who has invested their time, energy, money and focus to create a business that will succeed and provide you your desired return. As an early investor, you understand the business that you are in, in terms of where you fit in the marketplace, and you have a compelling vision of where the business will be when it achieves it's maximum level.

More importantly, you understand who the customers are, you know what the benefits, wants and needs the business provides these customers and you know where the money is, how to get it and how to spend and grow the money earned. You have a clear understanding as to the strengths and weaknesses of both yourself and that of your team; you know what resources the business needs and have a plan on how to gain these resources.

And lastly, you completely understand the risks involved with the business, from running and operating the business to serving your customers—you know what the risks are and have a way to manage it.

If you focus on being your business's most intelligent, wise and informed investor, you will know when its time to seek outside investment. You will know what terms are both reasonable and fair to you and your business. You will be able to attract the right Investor(s) with the right terms at the right time. You will be able to see the potential value that can be created by partnering with this company or that, because you are an Investor first and a business person second.

That's it. Seek investment for your company, as an Investor, not a business owner. Business owners have to care about the business's resources (people, equipment, etc.), they have to operate from a drive to provide outstanding service or product or whatever. Investors on the other hand (of which you are one) have to care about the risk and the return on their investment. The best investors invest for technical reasons not emotional ones, whereas some of the best entrepreneur's operate for both logical and emotional reasons. For investors, it's about the return, for business owners it's about *freedom and purpose.*

The most successful investors look for the following things when considering an opportunity:

- **RISKS & PROBABILITIES:**
  What are the risks?
  What is the probability that I will see a return-on-investment?
  What is the probability of 100% loss of investment?
  Do the numbers accurately reflect the reality of the market space the venture is playing in?
  Is my investment simply a means for the principals to exit from the business?

- **VIABILITY**
  Does the founder(s) have what it takes to lead and operate this business?
  Does the business have a strong management team? If not, is there a sound plan for creating one?
  Are the market, and the venture's potential stake in that market large enough, to provide an adequate return?

- **TIMING**
  Is the concept leading edge or *bleeding-edge?* If so, is it too early to introduce to the market place?
  Is the concept occurring in a maturing or dying market? As a late-entry, are they too late?

- **USE OF FUNDS ("Proceeds")**
  Is the business "on fire?" Meaning, are they seeking money to meet payroll/pay bills or to fund growth?

If investment is meant to fund growth, is it sufficient, or have they underestimated funding needs?

Financing Stages

What follows is a brief description of the stages of a business as taught at the Harvard Business School.[1]

Seed Financing: is the earliest stage of funding. A small investment (typically $25,000 to $300,000) is made to support an entrepreneur's exploration of an idea. Often there is no business plan, an incomplete management team, and little assurance that the basic technology or business concept is feasible. Sometimes, when the product technology is well established, seed money is raised simply to finance the recruitment of key management and the writing of business plan, both of which are generally necessary for start-up funding. Seed investors expect to provide basic business advice, and perhaps even office facilities, for their entrepreneurs. Seed investors often apply discount rates* of over 80 percent to the projects in which they invest.

* Discount Rate is the amount of return on investment that is expected. For example, let's say that a VC firm has a discount rate of 100 percent per annum. That means that the investment is must project to produce a return of 100 percent per year, compounded, on each $1 million investment in the company until the exit date (sale or IPO). Therefore, if the exit date is five years after the investment and

---

[1] From Daniel R. Scherlis and William A. Sahlman, "A Method for Valuing High-Risk, Long-Term Investments: The 'Venture Capital Method,'" note 288-006. Boston: Harvard Business School, 1987.

the investment is $1 million, the investor expects to receive $32 million upon a sale or an IPO. Bottom line: the longer you can put off seeking outside capital the cheaper it is for you both in terms of the return and dilution of equity.

Start-Up Financing: entails the commitment of more significant funds to an organization that is prepared to commence operations. A start-up should be able to demonstrate a competitive advantage. most high-technology firms should have a product in prototype form embodying a proprietary technology. A research-oriented venture, such as a biotechnology firm, might instead exhibit an impressive research staff. Low-technology ventures, such as specialty retailing or entertainment, should have a powerful concept with preemption advantages and a superior management. Investors in start-up ventures frequently provide assistance to management in recruiting key personnel, establishing sound management practices, and providing access to suppliers, banks and potential customers. Start-up investors apply discount rates of 50 percent to 70 percent.

First-Stage Financing: is provided to on-going businesses. A first-stage company is generally not profitable, but is normally has an established organization, a working product, and preferably some revenues. First-stage funds are usually used to establish a company's first major marketing efforts, and to hire sales and support personnel in anticipation of higher sales volume. Often, funds are also applied to product enhancements or product line expansion. First-stage investors attempt to monitor closely a venture's head count, ensuring that staffing levels correspond to attainable sales levels. They often become more actively involved as problems develop in production or sales and are prepared to replace key managers as necessary, sometimes filling in key positions themselves while searching for new managers. Discount rates applied to a first-stage venture are generally 40 percent to 60 percent.

Second-Stage Financing: is typically provided for working capital and fixed asset needs to support the growth of a company with active production, sustainable sales, and preferably, some profits. Whereas earlier-stage funds were largely dedicated toward proving a venture's viability, second- and later-stage capital is oriented toward the expansion of a tested contender. Since the capital invested in the later stages is more likely to pay for assets rather than operating expenses, it is more readily recoverable in the event of liquidation, thus lowering the overall risk to investors. Second-stage investors do not generally expect to become actively involved in problem solving as often as first-stage investors do. They do monitor performance closely, generally by comparison to a business plan. Discount rates for second-stage investments range from 30 percent to 50 percent.

Bridge Financing: is intended to carry a company until its IPO. Although an IPO is not yet appropriate due to market timing or the size and performance of the company, it is generally expected within a year after the bridge. Bridge investors might provide funds to satisfy ongoing capital needs, with the expectation of selling out again in the IPO as part of a secondary offering (an offering of shareholders', as distinct from company, stock). Alternately, bridge investors might apply some or all of their funds to buy out early-stage investors who are anxious to liquidate their holdings. Such an investor often expects to hold the stock past the IPO date, as a long-term investment. Bridge investors are generally passive investors. They apply discount rates of 20 percent to 35 percent.

Restart Financing: also known as emergency or sustaining financing, is raised for a troubled firm, at a price significantly below that of the previous round. Although the venture is performing well below expectations, the round will be priced low enough to offer a high-expected rate of return, one result of which is likely to be substantial dilution of any previous investors that do not participate in the restart financing.

Internal Rate of Return

The following table provides a "rule of thumb" for the internal rate of return required by professionally management venture capital funds.

Description	Internal Rate of Return
Seed/Start-up	60 – 100%
Development + Mgmt. Team	50 – 60%
Revenues/expansion	40 – 50%
Profitable/cash –poor	30 – 40%
Rapid growth	25 – 35%
Bridge to cash out (exit)	20 – 35%

Angel Investors

For many of you, Angel investors may be a good option over venture capital groups. In general, Angel investors are high-net-worth individuals who are willing to invest in developing enterprises. Of the approximately $50 billion in angel capital invested in the United States in 1997, $40 billion supposedly came from friends and family and was primarily invested in small, privately-held businesses (also known as "3F money," for friends, family and fools.)

Angel investors come from all walks of life and range from the unsophisticated investor (sometimes referred to as "recreational investors") who happens to like or believe in a particular entrepreneur or business to the sophisticated angel who views the investing as a business.

The unsophisticated angel investor typically purchases either common stock or high-yield notes (convertible or with warrants) and rarely set restrictions on the entrepreneur as to how the capital is used. They are sufficiently wealth so that the loss of the entire investment would not seriously affect them any more than a gambling loss would.

The sophisticated angel investor tends to purchase preferred stock or convertible notes and never common stock, so they will always be senior to the entrepreneur who holds common stock. They tend to conduct a significant amount of due diligence effort, and only invest in businesses they fully understand. Entrepreneurs should expect significant operating restrictions in any agreement with sophisticated angels.

You might be asking yourself: Where do I find an angel investor? In general, you find angels through networking. As Angel investors typically invest in businesses locally, your best bet might be to check around with your local bank, CPA's in the area who deal with investors and other business people, even your local church.

While there are now many web sites that offer resources to finding Angel investors, use them with caution. Three sources that I personally like and trust are:

The Kaufman Foundation
http://www.kauffman.org
eVenturing Site: http://www.eventuring.org
The Entrepreurship Research Portal: http://research.kauffman.org
Business EKG: http://businessekg.org (Free business benchmarking tool)
Kauffman Signature Series:
http://www.kauffman.org/signatureseries (Site dealing with business growth challenges)

U.S. Small Business Administration's ACE-NET
(The Angel Capital Electronic Network)
 www.sba.gov/advo

Small Business Investment Companies (SBICs)
c/o Associate Administration for Investment
U.S. Small Business Administration
409 3rd Street, S.W.
Washington, D.C. 20416
(202) 205-7589

Other Sites of Interest

Maximum Balance (Personal Development)

www.maximumbalance.com

MyBizHomepage.com (A free site for entrepreneurs seeking to gain control over their business finances and access to money)

www.mybizhomepage.com

Allbusiness.com (A fantastic information-site for Entrepreneurs)

www.allbusiness.com

John Asher Training (Master Sales Strategies from one of the World's best)

www.ashertraining.com

CHAPTER IX:

Striking A Balance in Business and Life

"Most people live, whether physically, intellectually, or morally, in a very restricted circle of their potential being. They make use of a very small portion of their consciousness, and of their soul's resources in general."
~ *William James*

Living a life in balance...

Leading a dynamic enterprise can sometimes be all consuming at times. It's all too easy to spend 10, 12, 15 hours in any given day focused on the affairs of the business. And what of your personal life? Do you seem to "sleepwalk" through dinners with the spouse? Do you go on automatic pilot, as you dutifully play with your children? If the answer is yes—yours is a life that is not in balance.

Granted, I do not know you personally, but if you are an entrepreneur or an intrapreneur—or any degree of risk taker, then we do indeed know one another. There is a connection, and it is that we seek to define our own purpose and establish freedom-- freedom to live our lives on our terms and to control or direct our destiny in a civilized society. Wealth is a key factor to attaining this freedom.

But freedom must first occur in the mind and the heart. Blind pursuit of money for money's sake is a disastrous strategy. It is a trap of enormous proportion and scale-one in which freedom is never truly attained. Instead, money is generated and it only buys you things—transactions, physical comforts, experiences and privileges—but it leaves you just a bit short. It doesn't provide true connection; it doesn't provide contentment and fulfillment.

Having nice things is very satisfying, but this satisfaction has a short life—it is fleeting, sometimes right after you've driven that new car off the lot or signed the deed on that new house.

> True satisfaction and fulfillment simply
> isn't for sale—at any price.

And therein lies the dilemma for many who've figured out the money game and nothing else. But you and I know better, right?

In the title of this book, I talk of cracking the code to massive wealth and the code is simply this: You must find a way to live a live that is meaningful and driven by a higher purpose than mere material pursuit.

If you really want to have an extraordinary life, filled with massive wealth in your personal and professional life, become obsessed with developing close, meaningful relationships, contributing to your community, becoming more self-aware, compassionate, grateful and generous with those around you.

One of the spiritually richest women the world has ever known was Mother Theresa. She gave of herself extensively; her focus was on the general well being of others. In return, the world gave her access to whatever resources she needed; she had access to every world leader, could make seemingly outrageous demands—and have them met. By all rights, she was a woman of enormous social wealth, who was devoted to living her life with purpose—a purpose that on many occasions impacted the world on a global scale.

As entrepreneurs, as savvy businessmen and women that I know you to be, this perhaps is the greatest task we can really be faced with (myself included.) To have a goal of say, becoming a millionaire is incomplete. As important as it is to know *what it is you want in your life* and how to get it, it's infinitely more important to understand *why you want it.* You have to know the *reasons*, and they must be compelling.

Real wealth, is the culmination of living well *while* happily achieving wealth. American businesspeople are especially prone to fall victim to the work ethic, to making one's professional lives a priority over one's personal life. I believe this is changing slowly. A millionaire, with outstanding business acumen but poor personal relationships is one of the poorest of souls.

The last lesson is the lesson of focus and purposeful living. Your interest, effort and focus on your professional endeavors and your personal life have to be equal. Both must be of equal importance for you to thrive in either.

Some of you may be thinking: "I can't possibly devote equal time and importance to both!" Well, we know that isn't true. How is it that you can meet and solve the most challenging problems in your professional world, find reserves of energy when none existed before—and not be able to succeed in your personal life?

When you say, "I can't," you are really saying: "I value one over the other, and I won't."

I'm here to tell you that they are both equal in importance to your overall happiness and contribution to the world. So, assume that I am correct-just take a moment and side with me on this. Here's what you stand to gain...

Better Health

By focusing on things that are important and un-urgent, focusing on things that you can control and influence, you create the right conditions for mind and body to work in a peak state towards your outcomes. A lot of people obsess over the very things that they can't control or influence. It is life draining, health threatening and ultimately futile to expend one's energy and focus on these things. Instead, focus on the things that are within your control and influence and ignore the rest. If you have to worry at all, worry upon things that are within your realm of influence.

A few important definitions:

Abundance:
Derived from Latin abundãre, meaning "to overflow"

Wealth:
Derived from the Old English *wel* or *welm*, meaning "well" or "well being." Well (weal) is to wealth as heal is to health.

Prosperity:
Derived from the Latin prosperãre, meaning "to render fortunate."

Affluence:
Derived from the Latin affluẽns, meaning "flowing."

Rich:
Derived from the Old English *rice*, meaning "strong," powerful."

With Better Health, More Energy

Health, Wealth and Energy are all interlinked. Your health is the *kingpin* to all actions that you take or don't take. In every case, the quality of your health determines the level of energy that you have to spend

Without energy, nothing good can be created or truly enjoyed. What's the point of achieving monetary wealth, only to be drained, devoid of the energy necessary to truly enjoy ones life? If there has been one area in my life that I've really failed at it would be in this area of health.

Fortunately for me, the demands of being a risk taker literally requires that massive amounts of energy be readily available. The price for achievement is paid for in Energy. Those with the best health enjoy the most wealth. Once you accept this, then working towards having great health becomes easy. If you find yourself having to lose weight, you no longer look upon this as losing anything, but instead, you are *gaining a better life.*

With More Energy, Quality of Relationships
& Time Increases

With more energy at your command, you just simply enjoy everything more. You're more pleasant to be around, and those closest to you will respond in kind. That's employees, partners, spouses, children, friends—everyone is impacted, and life is just better.

With more energy, you will be more willing to do the things that must be done vs. make excuses or create delays. With more willingness, more things get done, get done right and done in a timely manner. This leaves you with excess time to do what you enjoy doing. How so you ask? Simple: because you are willing to get things done vs. delay doing them, you no longer need to spend time dwelling on or thinking about that thing that you know you're supposed to get done. So you don't waist precious time giving it another thought.

People who procrastinate pay the highest price; not only do they not get what they themselves know is important done, they spend a great deal of mental energy thinking about it. Realize that there is no escape—time is spent, whether thinking about a thing or doing it— just do it.

The WealthDNA Life Wheel:

The life wheel is a fast and easy way of creating a snapshot of how you are doing in all the major areas of your life. Understand, that it is in constant motion, but by investing a few minutes know to plot out your life wheel, you will know the areas that need more energy, time and focus from you.

Take a few moments and, using the Life Wheel, starting from the center (0%), shade in the percentage that you believe you invest time and focus.

For example, here is what mine used to look like just a few years ago:

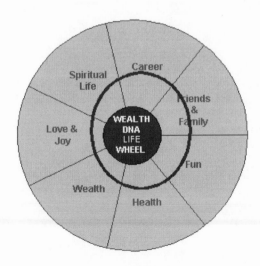

As you can see, I still had a great deal of work to do in the areas of Love & Joy, Spiritual Life and Health and Wealth categories. Practically all of my energy and focus was in the Career area, and very little attention was given to the internal needs of love and connection.

Notice that very little was generated in my primary goal area, Wealth, and with very little love and joy in my life, I was subjected to making great choices—and lousy choices. For many years, this pattern held true. I'd make great strides and achieve major objectives, only to see it mysteriously blow up.

The reasons are clear to me today—blindly achieving without the anchors and grounding of a whole life is simply an accident waiting to happen. And I'll tell you there were many accidents...

And here it is today:

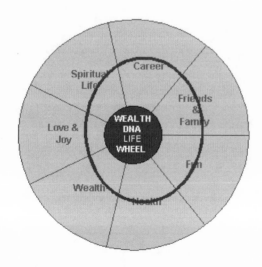

As you can see, there has been major improvement in the Health and Fun categories. Once I accepted the fact that wealth cannot occur in a vacuum, and that wealth was more than just money, everything improved. I was able to temper my career ambitions with the grounding that comes from actively nurturing my relationships and seeking out experiences that were fun and which brought joy to my life.

Being happier, having a fuller life, allowed me to genuinely feel grateful for the wealth I already had. And as a result of this gratitude, I've become very attractive to even more wealth. Even though there is still some imbalance in the areas of Love, Joy and health, I'm successfully moving towards creating outstanding health, and because I now understand what I will gain from this, it has never been easier. Great health=more energy=more everything…

Take a moment and think about what your Life Wheel looks like:

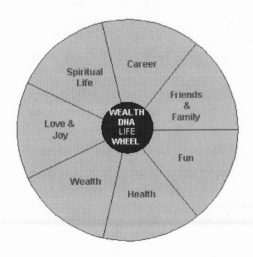

In what areas do you see that you could improve upon?

What would it mean to you to have more energy and focus in those areas? Instead of looking at having to sacrifice your time energy and focus in one area, ask yourself: What do I gain by placing more emphasis and effort in these areas?

Would focusing more energy or time or focus in a particular area create new results in other areas? If so, what might this look like?

Spend some time with the Life wheel. Really take the time to understand how investments in one area impact other areas of your life. They are all interlinked, and realizing this, you will find it easier to take the time to spend quality moments with friends and family, to make the investment in building or maintaining great health. What once was seen as a burden now becomes effortless.

In my travels, I've run across a great resource that deals directly with living life in balance. The company is called: Maximum Balance and they offer a free online community for us stressed out achievers to come in and decompress. Please take a moment of your time and go to:

www.maximumbalance.com Their content is spectacular and there's something for everyone here. To learn more about this and other programs offered, simply send an email to info@maximumbalance.com, and let them know you're a WealthDNA reader to receive the latest special discounts.

Ladies and Gentlemen, it's been quite a journey together. It has been a privilege and an honor to walk by your side as you've read these pages. I hope that this has been an enlightening and enjoyable experience. I know for me, it has been quite a life changing experience for me to create this work. And it's readers like yourselves that's made it all possible.

I wish each of you continued success along life's journey, and if you have any questions or comments to share, please email me at:

wealthdna@gmail.com

Chris

AFTERWORD

I wrote this book to give you the means to become not only an outstanding intrapreneur or entrepreneur, but also an exceptional one.

Now that you understand what the basic DNA of a Master Entrepreneur and Superior enterprise is comprised of, use this understanding and become one!

It is your right to achieve all that you dream about. You have all that you need right now to begin creating the life and destiny that you want for yourself and your loved ones right now.

No more excuses, no more delays, no more fear. It's time to create that extraordinary life, a life filled with wealth, purpose and joy.

Also, if you would like to be included in our mailing list, to be notified of other upcoming books in this series or others, please feel free to contact me at Wealthdna@gmail.com

ABOUT THE AUTHOR

Lee Christopher Grant spent the last 18 years mastering his entrepreneurial skills. Mr. Grant is the founder and CEO of Wealthgate, LLC, a niche consulting firm specializing in providing business consulting services to early-stage and emerging-growth companies. A serial entrepreneur, Mr. Grant has been involved in several ventures ranging from a music production company to a financial services firm, and in January of 2008, co-founded The Prosperity Fund, a private-equity fund based on Islamic finance.

He was the Chief Strategy Officer with Envision U, Inc., a personal development-training firm and co-founder of Firm Foundation Technology AEC, Inc., an Atlanta-based architectural-engineering-construction firm. Mr. Grant served as Acting Comptroller in General DataComm's Corporate Finance division.

A former Microsoft certified systems engineer, contributing author to Microsoft Certified Professional Magazine and technical consultant, he has over 20 years progressive experience in enterprise management and small business development, including; business analysis, finance, marketing, and product development. Mr. Grant has provided management and other consulting services to organizations such as Verizon Communications, GlobalOne, U.S. Postal Service, Smithsonian Institution and KPMG-Peat Marwick.

Mr. Grant currently serves on the advisory board for Harry F. Byrd School of Business, Institute for Entrepreneurship, Shenandoah University and has frequently lectured there. His commitment to the success of others, knowledge of the business development process and passion for personal growth are driving forces in his life. Chris has the extraordinary ability to take very dense and complex business situations and navigate his clients towards powerful and elegantly simple solutions.

Being involved with exceptional enterprises is a major passion for him, one he fulfills by serving on the boards of several dynamic companies. When he isn't influencing businesses or strategizing solutions, you can find him with friends and family, hiking, traveling, creating music or enjoying his antique flute collection. He lives in the United States, Virginia.

2984762

Made in the USA